DICTATION

(New Plays, Poems, and Monologues for African Americans)

Take note...   we've got something to say!

LaRita Shelby

Dictation

1st Edition

By LaRita Shelby

Published by: Sea To Sun Books
                 13547 Ventura Blvd. #678
                 Sherman Oaks, California 91423
                 (818) 942-2205 ext. 0016
                 www.sea2sun.com seatosun@qrio.com

Library of Congress Control Number: 2001118016

Shelby, LaRita

    New plays, poems, and monologues for African Americans.
    Dictation also includes the one acts Espresso Cafe and
    What A Man's Gotta Do and Greased, Fried and Laid
    to the Side, a play in two acts.

ISBN 0-9712021-2-5

SEA TO SUN BOOKS STANDARD ACCESS NUMBER: 2 5 3 - 9 5 5 1

ACKNOWLEDGMENTS

I'D LIKE TO DEDICATE THIS BOOK TO ALL THE WRITERS IN THE HAWKINS FAMILY. ONE DAY I DISCOVERED THAT THIS GIFT HAD ALREADY BEEN GRANTED. I AM JUST FORTUNATE ENOUGH TO CARRY ON.

TO AUNT MARY FOR ALL THOSE TIMES I WITNESSED YOUR ORATION OF THE CREATION, DIFFICULT AND DETERMINATION AND 'THEY SAY THE MASTER'SCOMING.' IT WASN'T UNTIL I WAS IN COLLEGE THAT I BECAME AWARE OF YOUR WRITING SKILLS, I STILL HAVEN'T FORGOTTEN YOUR BOOK OF POEMS.

TO AUNT RITTA (MY ELDEST AUNT) YOU ARE ONE OF THE MOST CREATIVE WOMEN I KNOW. THANKS FOR SHARING YOUR PERSONAL NOTE OF THANKS FROM ELEANOR ROOSEVELT, WHEN YOU WROTE A SPECIAL POEM FOR THE PRESIDENT WHILE YOU WERE STILL A YOUTH. I ALSO KEEP A COPY OF YOUR 'I CAN' POEM THAT WAS PUBLISHED IN THE YOUNG PEOPLES JOURNAL IN 1945. I CAN'T TELL YOU ENOUGH HOW MUCH I ALSO APPRECIATE YOUR SHARING A COPY OF A POEM WRITTEN BY MY MOTHER FLORENCE WHILE AT BOOKER T. WASHINGTON HIGH SCHOOL.

TO AUNT SUE, THANKS FOR MAKING ME LAUGH. PEOPLE THINK I'M FUNNY BUT YOU ARE THE REAL McCOY! TO STERLING AND RAY, THANKS FOR BEING MY BROTHERS. TO UNCLE WALTER, I LOVE YOU SO AND THANKS FOR THE CONSTANT ENCOURAGEMENT. ALSO MUCH LOVE TO STERLING, JR. TONY, J.J., SMITTY, MIKE, KAY, MARQUELINE, D. J., MARTIN AND MARCUS.

TO MY COUSIN REV. REGINALD PORTER, YOUR BOOK "WORDS FOR THE JOURNEY" WAS SO INSPIRING AND ANOTHER TESTAMENT OF OUR FAMILY LEGACY.

TO ROD, THANKS FOR ALWAYS MAKING ME THINK, EVEN AS A YOUNG GIRL YOUALWAYS APPEALED TO THE INTELLECTUAL APPROACH AND THANKS FOR HONORING MY GOOD REPORT CARDS. I'M SO PROUD OF YOU.

TO MY COUSIN ONCE REMOVED RICKY McKNIGHT BEST WISHES WITH YOUR SCRIPT. MAMA GREEN NEVER TOLD ME THAT YOU HAD SUCH SKILLS!

TO BETTY HUMMIL, MY LANGUAGE ARTS TEACHER AT CLARK ELEMENTARY SCHOOL. I STILL HAVE THE SPIRAL NOTEBOOK THAT YOU GAVE ME WHEN I WAS IN THE FIFTH GRADE. YOU TOLD ME TO KEEP WRITING AND I DID. I DIDN'T UNDERSTAND ITS POWER UNTIL NOW.

TO ALL OF MY SONGWRITING BUDDIES WHO TOOK THE TIME TO HEAR WHAT I WAS HEARING AND FEEL WHAT I WAS FEELING, I THANK YOU FROM THE BOTTOM OF MY HEART. THE WORDS STILL FLOW AND I STILL HEAR THE MUSIC. I PRAY THAT TIME GRANTS ME THE CHANCE TO ALSO LEAVE THE GIFT OF MUSIC.

TO MAMA NIKKI AND JUNEY SMITH, YOUR CONTINUED ENTHUSIASM OVER MY WRITINGS HAVE GIVEN ME WINGS. I'M READY TO FLY NOW, THANKS TO YOU.

TO VERNE', JUST COUNTING A WONDERFUL ACTRESS LIKE YOU AMONG MY FRIENDS IS A TREASURED ENDORSEMENT.

TO MOM "C" I UNDERSTAND WHAT THE STOOP IS NOW. I RE-WROTE THE POEM. TO DR. MAYME CLAYTON THANKS FOR PRESERVING OUR HISTORY VIA THE WESTERN STATES BLACK RESEARCH CENTER.

TO SY RICHARDSON, I WAS TEN FEET TALL WHEN YOU ASKED ABOUT MY LATEST WRITINGS. WELL HERE THEY ARE.

TO MY SON JUSTIN, THANK THE HEAVENS FOR BLESSING ME WITH YOU. IN YOUR EYES, I SEE MY EYES AND ALL THE HOPE FOR A NEW GENERATION. THANK YOU FOR SHOWING ME THAT I AM STRONGER THAN I EVER THOUGHT I WAS.

TO MY EXTENDED FAMILY DORIE, LEXI, VENUS, KEENA, AMANDA, TIFFANY, BRIAN, ANDREA AND VIDA I NEED YOU ALL AND I LOVE YOU ALL.

TO MY OTHER FAMILY, MY ACTING AND PERFORMING BUDDIES WHO ARE STILL CLIMBING, KEEP THE FAITH. KIM, KYM, ALEXIA, JENNIFER, REGGIE, BONITA, LICIA, INA, FELICIA, JANICE, WENDY, KELLITA AND TSHELENE. HOLLYWOOD HAS NO JUSTICE IF YOU DON'T GET YOUR DUE.

TO MY AGENTS AT MEDIA ARTISTS GROUP IT'S BEEN A LONG HAUL, WE'LL SEE WHAT THE NEXT RUNG WILL BE. MANY THANKS.

HEY MURIEL, REMEMBER WHEN I USED TO BE IN SCHOOL PLAYS, WELL I'M WRITING THEM NOW.

TO KAREN ROBERTS WHO MADE THE INITIAL JOURNEY WITH ME INTO THE MOUNTAINS. OUR FASTING AND PRAYING HAS PAID OFF. I WISH YOU THE BEST WITH YOUR SINGING AND SONGWRITING.

SPECIAL THANKS TO STAFFORD AND LYDIA FLOYD, LAVETA WALTON-RICE, GAIL Q. GIBSON AND JANICE WILLIAMS.

LOVE AND RESPECT IS THINE ALWAYS TO MY PRIMARY ARTISTIC NAVIGATOR THAT HELPED ENFORCE RESTORATION. THANK YOU.

TO ALL OF LIFE'S UNSAVORY MOMENTS, TO THE NAYSAYERS AND CRITICS... YOUR STAINS AND PAINS HAVE COLORED MY WORK AND GIVEN FLIGHT TO MORE AMBITION THAN YOU COULD EVER IMAGINE. THANK YOU FOR A NEW LAYER OF STRENGTH AND DETERMINATION.

TO MY HEAVENLY FATHER, THANK YOU FOR THE GIFT AND THE CALLING TO ENLIGHTEN AND INSPIRE.

DEDICATION

IT'S BEEN A FOUR YEAR JOURNEY SINCE I FIRST OPENED MY HEART TO WRITE THIS BOOK. IT COMES OUT OF THE CHANGING TIDES OF MY LIFE AND FROM THE WINDOWS OF MY SOUL. FROM THE PURE TO THE PROFANE THESE WRITINGS REFLECT TRACES OF ME AND TRACES OF THE WORLD THAT I SEE. THIS IS WHERE WE LIVE IN THE PRESENT TIME.

THESE WRITINGS ARE FOR A NEW CENTURY OF PERFORMERS.   HAVE FUN AND FILL THESE WORDS WITH YOUR BREATH AND YOUR OWN UNIQUE EXPERIENCES.

TABLE OF CONTENTS

For Women (continued)

59.	QUIRKS, WE'VE ALL GOT 'EM
61.	AIR FRESHENER
62.	FELLOWSHIP
63.	ALL MY MAMA'S
66.	WHEN I DIE I WANT TO BE OOOOLD!
68.	THAT'S OKAY HE'S MY BABY
70.	RAPE IS THE ISSUE
72.	MILLION MAN MARCH
73.	MY THIGH MOVED
75.	ANGRY BLACK WOMAN'S POEM
76.	TALK SHOW AUDIENCES/THAT IS NOT US!
77.	THE LATITUDES OF ATTITUDES (FEMALE VERSION)
78.	WHITE GIRLS AND BLACK GUYS
80.	DIFFERENT KIND OF BLACK MAN
82.	NEVER MIND
83.	TRUST
84.	BAGGAGE CLAIM IS TO THE LEFT
85.	SOMEONE MURDERED JUNE CLEVER
86.	MY BUTT DROPPED
87.	I'M SORRY MRS. PHELPS
88.	I'M SORRY ANGRY BLACK WOMAN
90.	HELP MY TODDLER'S TRYING TO KILL ME
91.	NO APOLOGIES
92.	CALLING FORTH BOOM SHENANA SHAY SHAY
93.	READING & CHECKING

For Men

95.	LATITUDES OF ATTITUDES (MALE VERSION)
96.	IT'S IN MY WALK
97.	ANGRY BLACK MAN'S POEM
98.	SHE BROUGHT GREAT DRAMA
99.	HOOK A BROTHER UP
100.	CAUGHT
101.	HE JUST WASN'T
102.	HE WAS BUT I WISH HE WASN'T
103.	HE WAS AND I'M GLAD HE WAS
104.	THE PROMOTION
105.	SHE WANTED ME TO MISS THE GAME
107.	SHE WAS ALL OVER ME
108.	IDENTITY

THE PLAYS

110.	ESPRESSO CAFE Dramatic 1 Act
	2 Characters, either sex or mixed cast.
120.	WHAT A MAN'S GOTTA DO 1 Act
	3 males, 3 females Romantic comedy
147.	GREASED FRIED AND LAID TO THE SIDE
	2 Acts 11 characters A comedy with a message.

Poems, Prose, Monologues and Scenes for Either Sex

THE LAKE

This morning I woke up by a beautiful lake with soft quiet ripples so peaceful and so serene. At first I just stood there staring and wondering how could something be so awesome and yet so simple? Just viewing the lake was like being lured under the control of a most skillful hypnotist. Instantly, my heart and mind were entranced by the tranquility of these slow moving waters. But then I thought, there is no hypnotist in the world that has this much power. My flesh tingled and the hairs on my arms immediately rose to attention as though saluting the presence of nature's chief officer. I could feel the Creator's embrace. I was the welcome guest and He was the most gracious host.

There sat such an elegant lake, high in the snowcapped mountains, encamped by towering pines that stood like a tribe of nature's warriors guarding a cool reservoir. As the winds gently blew, the trees seemed to bow and curtsy as a sign of respect to me, God's greatest creation. It was then that I truly realized that I have dominion over every living thing. My soul reminded me that I am a part of all creation and creation is a part of me. I trust nature to provide me with nourishment and shelter. In return, I have a duty to care for the land, the water and all other living creatures of the earth.

This lake was like a meeting place for me and the unseen proprietor to discuss his private agenda. I could hear the wisdom of the ages softly speaking in my ear. The voice said; "Tell them it is not by coincidence that they exist. Tell them that the earth is provided as a happy and healthy dwelling place. Tell them that man and nature co-exist and one cannot survive without the other."

Here beside this lake, I felt a sense of royalty that I had never experienced before amongst the octane and asphalt of city life. I felt like a divine high priestess (or priest) and my social, ethnic, political or economic status had nothing to do with it. This feeling was more rewarding than any man made set of virtues. Here I stood beside this lake, finally knowing that I was in tandem with every female (male) entity that was ever created and that I am part of a divine plan to nurture and give birth to (procreate) everything that is born from now until infinity. I'm part of that plan and I have something in common with every female (male) human being, mammal or fish. I am indeed the mother (a son) of the universe.

Be still and listen, there is wisdom in the waters. There is comfort and there is healing right there in the waters. Find your waters, touch them and let them soothe you. Quiet your own thoughts, and let the waters teach you. There is more than subtle ripples, there is more than cascading waves, there is something in the waters for you. Go. Find your waters and let the waters teach you.

PANS AND DISHES

Pans and Dishes is what I saw outside the temple that Sunday.

Blessed sisters draped in white baring such tasty delights.

Pans and Dishes from far and near in foil wrapped fragrant portions,

So satisfying to the soul and such delicious consumption.

Pans and dishes filled the conference table, the menu said potluck.

There's collard greens, spinach quiche and orange flavored duck.

There's other things I don't recognize from folks who don't look like they can cook.

I'll taste the greens, sample a few other things and as for the rest, I'll just look.

Pans and dishes filled the house and black was the color of the day.

There were so many sincere caterers but my taste buds had melted away.

Pans and dishes all over the kitchen but my favorite chef was not there.

And all the sweetest pies and cakes could not replace my heart's despair.

Pans and dishes have built a nation,

A few schools and churches too.

Pans and dishes from aunts and mammas

And just plain folks like you.

THE AUDITION

I'm here Hollywood, I'm ready for you to make me a star! Oh, excuse me for a moment the
telephone's ringing, it's probably my brand new agent calling. Hello? Oh hi Ralph. Uh, huh?
They're looking for my type? Its a series regular three year guarantee! It shoots on location!
Uh huh? The audition is tomorrow morning at 11:00 And the sides are available til five thirty at
The old MGM lot in Culver City. But its ten minutes to five o'clock now! Okay! Okay I'll hurry!
I'm on my way!! I'm gonna' get this part Ralph! All I need is a chance. You won't regret signing
me. I know can do it. I gonna' blow them away! In a year I'm going to be rich!! I'll finally be able
to buy my mama a house and my Uncle Bill won't have to drive a cab any more... Huh? Oh Yea, Yea,
I'm on my way!!
(Transition)

Well Hollywood, I've been here for a little while now and boy what a ride it has been.
It seems like it was just yesterday but its been more than ten years already. Oh excuse me, that's
the telephone.? Oh hey buddy! How was your blind date last night? Uh huh? Uh huh?
Wait a minute hold on. That's my other line. (clicking over) Hello? Oh hi Paul?! So you're
Ralph's new assistant? And he would like to speak to me? Uh huh? Oh Really? They want
to see me for a fourth call back?

(Not very enthusiastic) Great! Uh, listen?   Can you call me back later because I'm
on the other line right now? Okay, bye bye. (Clicking back over) I'm sorry that was my
agent. Now what were you saying?

.

SOMETIMES I LIKE SOUL FOOD

Sometimes I like to eat soul food! No, not at the fancy watered down places located in some posh restaurant row on the ritzy part of town. I mean down home, greasy, fat lady cooking, blues playin in the background Soul Food. I mean sometimes I like going to a restaurant where the cook has a picture on the wall with everybody that ever had a hit record back when Stax was a big time label. Sometimes I like hanging out in a place where the waitresses chew gum and call everybody "sugah" and "honey." Sometimes I like to see a waiter with food stains on his apron. And over seeing the whole joint is a large portrait of a big beautiful black woman with a flower in her hair and a loving smile that spans from cheek to cheek.

Sometimes I like to get cozy in an atmosphere where sopping is very fashionable. Sopping, for those who may not know, is when you take your last bit of corn bread, bun or biscuit and swipe the plate clean of any remaining sauce, juice or gravy. For those of you who have never experienced this, I suggest that you give it a try, the dishwasher will love you for it. Sometimes, I like going to a place where the line might be a little long on Sundays and parking might be a little scarce. But the trip is well worth it as long as there is the mention of "slapping your mama" or of someone having put his or her "foot in it." *It* being the food of course. Perhaps the true test of a soul food journey is whether or not you can make the ride home without unbuckling your belt. Bon Appetite.

*Note: Stax a major label back in the 1970's. Their biggest selling artists were Al Green, Sam and Dave and The Staple Singers. Phrases like "this food is so good, you'll want to slap your mama" or "the cook must have put his foot in it" have been used in our culture for many years, especially in the South.

I LEFT GENERATIONS SITTING ON THE STOOP

Have you ever gone back to the old neighborhood to find that some people haven't changed at all? They are still sitting there in front of their houses, playing dominos and drinking wine. They want to hear all about what you've done and where you've been but when you've finished telling them, they have nothing to say. You might even silently consider whether they're even happy for you at all or if they quietly resent you for having had the courage to venture out. Well, I left generations sitting on the stoop.

There's a few new faces on the scene. The offspring that they produce seem to grow up and do what they've seen their elders do and nobody moves away from home. The ones that were little babies when I left are teenagers and now they've got babies. As for the grown ups that were in their twenties and thirties, they are still there and some of them have had more babies. And the old folks that are still alive are also still there and nobody has left home. I left generations sitting on the stoop.

They look at me and their eyes tell me what they're thinking; "What makes her/him so different? I even ask myself sometimes what makes me different. It's not that I think I'm better than they are. Let's face it all of our ancestors came over on the same boats. And I'm from the same part of time and history that they are. But still it pounds on my heart just to realize that I left generations sitting on the stoop.

Where is the light, where is the growth and who will break this lethargic cycle? I wish that I could convince them that what they are looking for someone else to do, they can do for themselves. Deep down inside, I know they want more and deep down inside I wish I could give it to them. There are so many of my beautiful people merely existing from month to month and day to day. And these are the generations that I left sitting on the stoop.

SAYING GOOD-BYE

It was just a regular day at work. Nothing out of the ordinary was going on although I had a rather restless night the night before. The phone rang. It was for me. My aunt Rita was on the line. She said it was bad news and I forced her to tell me what it was. She did. She gave me the number to the Detroit coroner. "We found your mother dead in her home yesterday and we have her body, you have to come claim it." I was the next of kin. I didn't know where to begin. All I knew was that within twenty-four hours I had to be on a plane to do business in a strange city. It was time to say good-bye.

Friends and family gave so generously. I was unprepared for an unexpected funeral. The story of my mother and me was not typical but it was full of sincere love. You see for many years I waited for this dear woman to come back for the little brown pig tailed child that she left with Aunt Mary long ago but I never even knew of her pain. So when I finally decided to do the reaching, the gap had already grown too large. She always felt like she owed me more than what she had already given me and I always wanted to hit the big time just so that I could make life easier for her. But now it was time to say good-bye.

Mama never let me buy any clothes for her but today I was buying her a new dress. A friendly sales clerk asked me in a perky voice: 'May I help you?' "Why yes! I'm looking for something to match my mother's blue casket. Do you think this shade will do?" It was time to say good-bye.

I felt like I was in a vacuum. Even though there were people around I felt so all alone. I had to go into each of my mothers rooms and pack her whole life into a pile of boxes. How do you put someone's life in a box? And I thought, people have been going through this all the time, this is just the first time that it was happening to me. I stopped and looked down at my feet and there amongst the clutter was a photo of a brown, beautiful, big legged, high stepping majorette from Booker T. Washington High School. I had found mama's pride and joy!! But still, it was time to say good-bye.

I wish that there were some type of training. Something. Anything to brace you for this emptiness this incredible sense of loss that sometimes makes you feel like you're loosing your mind. There are those that happily say to you; "she's not really gone she's right there beside you" and I know that they mean well but I live in a three dimensional world with a three dimensional body and I surely miss that which I cannot see, feel or hold. I wish I'd learned back in kindergarten that some day I'd have to say good-bye. Good-bye Mama. Good-bye, wish I had known you better...but I couldn't have loved you more.

REGGIE, ME, ROLAND AND VC

IT WAS THREE DAYS BEFORE CHRISTMAS ON THE CRENSHAW STRIP
AND WE HAD ALL DECIDED ON CHICKEN
 IT WAS REGGIE, ME, ROLAND AND V.C.
AND WE'D GOTTEN INTO SOME SERIOUS FINGER LICKING.

 NOW THREE OF US HAD JUST LEFT A FUNERAL
AND WE COULDN'T BELIEVE OUR BOY LEXI WAS GONE
AND AS FOR ROLAND, HIS HOUSE HAD CAUGHT FIRE
FORTUNATELY AT THE TIME HE WASN'T AT HOME.

DAMN, THIS IS SOME KIND OF LUCK WE'RE HAVING
SUCH GRIEF AND CALAMITY, HAND IN HAND
JUST A FEW MORE DAYS BEFORE CHRISTMAS
BUT THIS WAS NO WINTER WONDERLAND

THREE STRONG MEN AND ONE TENACIOUS LADY
ON THE CRENSHAW STRIP IN THE COLONEL'S LOT
JUST SMACKING AND EATING CHICKEN
THEN I HAD A FUNNY THOUGHT;

'MAN DO YOU KNOW HOW MUCH CHICKEN LEXI MUST'VE EATEN
BEFORE THE DAY HE DIED?
HE WAS A HEFTY YOUNG MAN,
HE PROBABLY LIKED IT BAKED, SAUTÉED AND FRIED.'

AS SAD AS WE WERE, WE CHUCKLED
THIS WAS A DAY TO FORGET
AND JUST MAYBE LEXI WAS SOMEWHERE IN HEAVEN
CHOPPING DOWN ON A CHICKEN BREAST.

PEOPLE DIED SO I COULD VOTE

I am so busy today. It's getting late and I have a lot of things to do. The phone is ringing, deadlines are catching up with me and yet there's one very important thing I that I must take the time to do. I've got to go vote. Today is Election Day and for once I actually took the time to read the election pamphlet and study the issues so that I have a clear idea of what it is and who it is that I am voting on. Then it dawned on me, people died so that I could vote. A simple thing that most people take for granted is such a serious issue for me. When I truly think about it, it's rather sickening. The struggle for voting rights for African Americans didn't just take place a hundred years ago. It was still happening in my life time. Now I am a young adult but when I was born, it was illegal for my father to vote in the state of Mississippi, the state of his birth. That's your dirty laundry America. And I am also still amazed at how many foreigners come to this country with such a disrespect for African-Americans when it was us who bled and died for the amendments to the constitution that gave them the right to citizenship and the right to vote. It was us who had the dogs and the water hoses turned on us and it was us who took the blows from a squadron of brutal and hateful police. And there was no trial for that! There was no public outrage for the thousands of mysterious murders of innocent black folks who wanted to live a decent and productive life in the country that they helped to build for free! There were no radio talk shows of frustrated white collar workers who were so "upset" with the justice system. And this was all in my lifetime. People died do that I could vote. They *had* to die, so that their children and grand children could walk into the voting booth, pull the curtain and have a say in what happens in this country. So today I am going have my say.

LAVA LAMPS,

 SOAP ON A ROPE

AND CHIA PETS!

ONE WORD,

WHY?

> LAVA LAMPS,
>
> SOAP ON A ROPE
>
> AND CHIA PETS!
>
> TWO WORDS,
>
> FATHER'S DAY!

LAVA LAMPS,

SOAP ON A ROPE

AND CHIA PETS,

 THREE WORDS,

TAKE IT BACK!!

OH, WAIT A MINUTE *FOUR* WORDS

GET YOUR MONEY BACK.

> LAVA LAMPS,
>
> SOAP ON A ROPE
>
> AND CHIA PETS,
>
> OHH....THERE'S A LENGTHY MESSAGE COMING IN.
>
> AH, YES, HERE IT IS......TWELVE WORDS,
>
> 'DON'T ORDER FROM THE CABLE TV SHOPPING SHOW, GET A LIFE INSTEAD
>
> AND SPARE YOUR FRIENDS FROM PRETENDING THAT THEY UNDERSTAND
>
> WHY YOU GAVE THEM SUCH A GIFT!'

It always sat there on the coffee table. We were so excited every month to get a new one.

Who would be on the cover? Whose house would we get to see? What was the new fashion?

In addition to a picture of Jesus and Martin Luther King on the wall, every home had a subscription

to Ebony Magazine.

This month it was the anniversary issue. I couldn't wait to open it up! Who would make

this year's list of one hundred most influential blacks? I was eagerly flipping the pages and then I

saw something that disturbed me. I didn't know if I should put the book down and pretend that I didn't

see it or if I should just keep staring. I was only about ten years old and Ebony was such a happy

magazine, why would they just put this picture right there in the middle of the magazine without a

warning. It was a picture of a black man's body that had been charred. The caption said that his

name was Emmitt Till. He had been beaten to death and drug through the town because he whistled

at a white lady. I flipped the page. There were more pictures. There were pictures of men in white

sheets and they frightened me. Some of them were standing next to burning crosses. There were also

pictures of this church that was burned up and beside that picture were the pictures of four little girls

who had gone to Sunday School that Sunday but they never returned. I remember all of this. I saw all

of this in that magazine.

From time to time I heard a song about "Strange Fruit" by Billy Holiday but the song wasn't

about fruit at all. I was ten years old. Why were there pictures of these men hanging on trees. I looked

real hard to see their faces. I could see where there hands had turned stiff and their shirts had been

ripped off and some of them had whip marks across their backs. And standing all around was a sea of

white faces smiling as though they were at the circus or something. And this all happened here! In

Georgia, in Mississippi, in Alabama and maybe even right here? This all happened on American soil.

There is no ocean that separates us from our tribulations! There is no body of water that we have

crossed to leave all of this pain behind.

I closed the magazine and tried to forget about what I saw. I hid the magazine underneath

all the others because those pictures frightened me.   When I went to sleep that night, even though

the magazine was safely tucked in the bottom of the pile on Aunt Mary's coffee table, I saw those

pictures again.

As they say, I'm grown now. And I'm happily subscribed to Ebony and Jet. I got a new Jet magazine last week. On the cover was the world champion Chicago Bulls. Michael Jordan and Scotty Pippin were showing off those million dollar smiles. On the inside I saw another picture of a tree bearing strange fruit. The victim was nineteen year old Keith Warren. The date of his mysterious demise is July 1986. The family was seeking to have the case reopened. That night when I went to sleep, I saw all of those pictures again.

ARE THERE ANY HAPPY BLACK PEOPLE ON THE PLANET?

HELLOOOOO?!   HELLOO OUT THERE?!!

ARE THERE ANY HAPPY BLACK PEOPLE ON THE PLANET?

THAT'S WHAT I WANT TO KNOW!

OR IS EVERYBODY THAT'S NOT OUT PROTESTING

SITTING AT HOME IN A CORNER HUMMING NEGRO SPIRITUALS?

WHERE ARE ALL THE HAPPY PEOPLE?

YES I KNOW ABOUT THE STRUGGLE,

AND THE STRUGGLE CONTINUES

BUT IS ANYTHING NEW ABOUT THAT?

ARE THERE ANY HAPPY BLACK PEOPLE ON THE PLANET?

WHERE ARE ALL THE PEOPLE WHO ARE CAUGHT UP IN THE MUSIC OF LIFE!

WHERE ARE THOSE FIERCE GROUPINGS OF OUR KINSMEN

WHO SAY, TO HELL WITH THE SYSTEM

WE ARE GOING TO CELEBRATE ANYWAY!

ARE THERE ANY HAPPY BLACK PEOPLE ON THE PLANET?

I MEAN, WHERE ARE THOSE PEOPLE WHO SAY

"SINCE WE'RE HERE, WE MAY AS WELL HAVE SOME FUN!

WHERE ARE THOSE PEOPLE WHO SAY LIFE IS A DANCE!

ARE THERE ANY HAPPY BLACK PEOPLE ON THE PLANET?

WHERE ARE THE PEOPLE WHOSE ATTITUDE IS

"SHUCKS, AFTER ALL WE'VE BEEN THROUGH,

WE MUST BE INDESTRUCTIBLE! SO I'M HAVING A BALL!"

WHERE ARE THE HAPPY BLACK PEOPLE?

DO ANY LIVE ON THIS PLANET?

BUT SHE SAW THEM WITH HUMAN EYES

Her office sat in a trendy high rise in the heart of Beverly Hills. It was the perfect address for a budding talent agency. On any given day scores of talented and beautiful young people paraded in and out of the tiny suite all bearing tales of hometown victories. All eager to crack the nut that was known as Hollywood. These were L.A's newest citizens who were drawn by the glitter and the dream of tinsel town.

One by one they flooded the phone lines, they pounded the pavement they did whatever they could possibly do to give themselves *the edge.* They all wanted that certain something that would catapult them to instant stardom. They believed there was such a thing as "an overnight sensation." But she saw them with human eyes. The twinkle in her pupils was far more than they would ever get in most assembly line casting situations. Her piercing gaze was a loving and knowing insight that saw past their confident countenances. She saw their fear. She saw their desperation. They were desperate to be accepted. She saw that they had been coerced by the glare of bright lights and award shows. They thought that this would be a short and pleasant ride. She saw into their hearts and what she saw told her that they had no idea that they would encounter so much rejection. She felt their sincere passion but she knew that all the passion in the world would not pay a light bill or a phone bill or rent. She saw that they were so desperately seeking stardom, that many of them forgot to learn how to do anything else. Their whole existence was predicated on what happened in a casting session. She saw their glossy 8x10's, but she read more than their resumes could ever tell. She saw them with human eyes and she knew. *She knew.*

NORTH AND SOUTH

Northerner: I come from the cold great North, the Northeast United States. Hear my sophisticated tones, my extensive vocabulary and whisk away in my eclectic flair as I whip around corners of brown stone with the tails of my London Fog trailing in the icy breeze. Beneath my tightly clinched elbows lie The New York Times, The Wall Street Journal or the Chicago Tribune. My head is high my shoulders are erect and all non verbal posture indicates that I am far superior to anyone who falls beneath my geographic domain. This is the North and I am a Northerner.

Southerner: Raked over cotton fields, Dixie boarders and dirt roads are the stomping grounds upon which I call home. From the big house to the out house this is my history. These are my roots. Wheat fields and wooden mail boxes are perched from curb to curb. Southern dishes and delicacies have nourished the cast iron character and down home values that makes us folks so hospitable. The ghosts from torn down plantations meet the spirits of strange Southern fruit. Living rooms, big back yards and swings on creaky verandahs with rocking chairs have been the settings for my life's lessons. Dungarees and pick up trucks, bare feet, shot guns and fishing poles are the wardrobe and props for my inventions and traditions. The boats docked here, the marches began here and everybody branched out loosing their memories to their younger generations, this was home to them damn Yankees.

Northerner: Damn Southerners, so country, so common, so slow, so ignorant.

Southerner: Damn Northerners, so proper, so rude, so bourgeois and always in a hurry!

Northerner: Slow ass, back woods jigaboos..

Southerner: Always got their head up in the air looking down their nose at somebody...

Northerner: So country, just plain ass country, now they can just butcher The Queen's English...

Southerner: Like the Queen gives a damn about your ass, like she knows your address...

Northerner: At least she can find my address. I don't live in the back woods somewhere with all

of my cousins in a shot gun shack with chickens in the back.

Southerner: And you call that concrete jungle of yours a home? Blood stains, broken glass and black smog...

Northerner: I unequivocally despise the ignorance of your bravado and your pitiful state of prejudice.

Southerner: Prejudice? Do you actually think that the tonality of your voice and your choice of words displays any more intelligence? It only shows how far you've gone to assimilate and make sure that the vernacular doesn't slip out. What you have is a case of geographic prejudice.

Northerner: Damn you Southerner

Southerner: Damn you Northerner

Northerner & Southerner: DAMN!

ACTING LIKE A DAMN FOOL

HAVE YOU EVER BEEN GOING SOMEWHERE, DRESSED UP, LOOKING GOOD, SMELLING GOOD, FEELING GOOD AND SOMETHING WENT WRONG.   SOMETHING DIDN'T GO AS PLANNED. SOMEONE FELL BENEATH EXPECTATIONS AND THEN SUDDENLY BUT NOT SO UNEXPECTEDLY SOMEONE IN YOUR GROUP PROCEEDS TO RESPOND... TO PROTEST, TO PONTIFICATE. IN OTHER WORDS SOMEONE CHOOSES TO ACT LIKE A DAMN FOOL... AND THERE YOU ARE! PEOPLE ARE LOOKING, WHISPERING, MURMURING, MAYBE EVEN CHUCKLING BECAUSE YOU, YES YOU ARE THE ONE WITH *THE ONE* WHO'S ACTING LIKE A DAMN FOOL. YOU TRY TO REASON. YOU BEG FOR SUBTLETY.   YOU EVEN PLEAD FOR NO FURTHER EMBARRASSMENT BUT THIS ONLY INCITES MORE. .MORE VOLUME, MORE GESTURES, .MORE RECITATIONS OF "OH NO!! HELL NO!!! I'LL GO APE SHIT UP IN THIS MO-FO!! I DON'T GIVE A DAMN ABOUT THESE F'ING PEOPLE!"

THIS IS WHAT YOU HEAR ECHOING THROUGHOUT THE BUILDING AND NOW OF COURSE EVEN THOSE WHO WERE ON THE PARKING LOT ARE AWARE THAT SOMETHING IS DREADFULLY WRONG. THEY TOO NOW KNOW THAT SOMEWHERE INSIDE SOMEONE (SOME FOOL) IS ACTING LIKE A *DAMN* FOOL AND YES *YOU* ARE THE ONE WHO IS WITH THAT FOOL. WHAT'S WORSE, THAT FOOL IS THE ONE WHO'S DRIVING.

YES YOU RODE WITH *THAT FOOL* AND IF THE POLICE DON'T COME FIRST, YOU GOTTA DEPEND ON *THAT FOOL* TO GET YOU BACK HOME, OR AT LEAST TO HIS/HER HOUSE BECAUSE THAT'S WHERE YOU LEFT YOUR CAR. AFTER ALL YOU ARE THE SMART ONE THAT RODE WITH THAT DAMN FOOL IN THE FIRST PLACE.

OH THE SHAME, THE HUMILIATION, THE CONTEMPLATION BECAUSE IN A MERE HEARTBEAT THAT SAME FOOL WILL WANT TO START SOME SHIT WITH YOU AND THEY KNOW NOT TO *EVEN* GO THERE BECAUSE THEN THERE WOULD BE *TWO FOOLS* UP IN HERE AND LORD KNOWS THAT ONE FOOL IS MORE THAN ENOUGH.

VIOLENCE/ NON VIOLENCE: IN THE NAME OF PEACE

WHEN YOU TOLD ME YOUR PERCEPTION OF ME WAS TOO AGGRESSIVE
I OPTED FOR A MORE PASSIVE DEMEANOR. I CHOSE TO COOPERATE WITH THE SYSTEM
THAT YOU DESIGNED BUT STILL YOUR INNER AGGRESSIONS SURFACED AND YOU TURNED
YOUR VIOLENCE ON ME. I WAS THERE, IN YOUR KITCHEN COOKING YOUR FOOD, CLEANING
YOUR HOUSE, FEEDING YOUR BABY AND MAKING LOVE TO YOU IN OUR BEDROOM BUT YOU
BROUGHT THE PAIN FROM YOUR UNSOLVED GENERATIONS AND DELIVERED THEM TO ME WITH
FORCE AS THOUGH I WAS THE CAUSE.

I WAS THERE WORKING BESIDE YOU, MAKING SMALL TALK, SORTING MAIL KEEPING
OUT OF THE WAY OF YOUR ANXIETIES WITH THE BOSS BUT YOU RETURNED TO OUR STATION
AND STILL YOU TOOK IT OUT ON ME.

I WAS THE LITTLE CHILD THAT REMINDED YOU OF HIM; THE ONE THAT YOU HATED
AND THE ONE THAT HURT YOU. I LOVED YOU PURELY AND INNOCENTLY BUT STILL YOU
CHOSE ME TO ACT UPON TO FEED YOUR HABIT.

I TOO WAS BEHIND THE WHEEL OF THAT TAXI CAB, THE ONE THAT PICKED YOU UP
WHEN OTHERS PASSED YOU BY AND YOU DREW YOUR WEAPON ON ME, LEAVING ME
INCAPACITATED. I WAS THE ONE IN UNIFORM, THERE TO PROTECT YOUR NEIGHBORHOOD
BUT INSTEAD I CAUGHT YOUR BULLET.

I WAS THERE IN THAT LITTLE NATION, THAT HAD NOTHING TO DO WITH YOUR
POLITICAL SITUATION AND YES, YOU WIPED MY VILLAGE CLEAN, HOW COULD YOU BE
SO MEAN?

AND AS I REMEMBER, I WAS THERE IN THAT MARCH IN THE SOUTH, QUIETLY,
NON VIOLENTLY AND STILL YOU TURNED YOUR DOGS ON ME.

AND IF YOU WOULD ALLOW ME TO RECALL, I WAS THERE ON THAT SHIP,
ON THAT PLANTATION AND IN THAT COTTON FIELD, WORKING AND SLAVING FOR YOU
AND YET MY FREE LABOR WAS NOT ENOUGH, YOU WANTED TO SEE ME BLEED.

SO AS I AM ACTED UPON, I HAVE ALSO LEARNED TO ACT. I WAITED FOR YOU
TO TREAT ME JUSTLY BUT MY WAIT WAS IN VAIN. YOU TAUGHT ME ANGER AND VIOLENCE
AND LIKE THE GOOD STUDENT THAT I AM, I LEARNED. I LEARNED IT WELL.

YOU ROBBED FROM MY PEOPLE, SO NOW I ROB FROM YOU. YOU SHOW ME THAT THERE IS NO JUSTICE, I SHOW YOU THAT THERE IS NO PEACE. YOU LAUNCH YOUR EXPLOSIVES IN THE NAME OF PEACE. YOU LET YOUR PEOPLE CROSS THE BORDERS BUT KEEP MY PEOPLE OUT. WE ARE BROTHERS AND SISTERS IN SIN. VIOLENCE AND NON/VIOLENCE ARE SIAMESE TWINS. WHERE DO WE SEPARATE, WHERE DO WE BEGIN. IF I ABIDE BY, LIVE BY AND SWEAR BY NON VIOLENCE, CAN I SOMEHOW KILL MY SIAMESE TWIN?

HERE'S TO THE ARTIST

HERE'S TO THE ARTIST. HERE'S TO THE ONES WHO HAVE STAYED IN THE BUSINESS OF CREATING ART.

TO THE ONES WHO DRAFT PICTURES TO SEE, POEMS TO READ, MOVIES TO WATCH, AND ART TO ENJOY.   TO THE ACTORS, THE EXTRAS, THE VISIONARIES.

TO THOSE WHO CREATE MUSIC TO LISTEN TO, DANCE TO, OR IGNORE.

FOR EVERYONE WHO'S EVER ENDURED A CONVERSATION WITH YOUR MOTHER, YOUR GRAND MOTHER, COUSIN OR IN LAW WHILE THEY EDGE UP ON QUESTIONS LIKE , "YOU KNOW JOE PHILLIPS HAS BEEN AT THE POST OFFICE SINCE HIGH SCHOOL AND HE'S ABOUT READY TO RETIRE AND BUY HIS SECOND HOUSE."

THEN THESE OBVIOUS AND OBLIVIOUS RELATIVES CONTINUE WITH, "DID YOU EVER THINK ABOUT BEING A SCHOOL TEACHER?"

 OR FOR THOSE WHO LACK ANY ARTISTIC REVERENCE AT ALL AND JUST COME OUT AND ASK "WHEN ARE YOU GOING TO GET A REAL JOB?"

THIS ODE IS TO YOU, THE ARTIST THAT HAS ENDURED.

THIS IS FOR THOSE WHO CAN'T JUST WALK AWAY FROM IT. IT'S FOR THOSE WHO DEAL WITH THE UNEXPLAINABLE GNAWING FEELING THAT SOMETIMES CUTS LIKE A KNIFE AND AT OTHER TIMES IT FEELS LIKE A BOMB ABOUT TO BURST INSIDE OF YOU UNLESS YOU WRITE, YOU PAINT, YOU DRAW, YOU ACT, YOU DANCE, YOU SING, YOU CONSTRUCT, YOU COMPOSE, YOU PLAY, YOU PERFORM!!

THIS TRIBUTE IS FOR THOSE WHOSE JOB DESCRIPTION DOES NOT NECESSARILY APPEAR IN THE SUNDAY TIMES, THE DAILY NEWS OR THE WEEKLY TRIBUNE.

THIS IS FOR YOU, WHOSE WORK HISTORY WILL NEVER DESCRIBE THE LIVES THAT HAVE BEEN TOUCHED, THE HEARTS THAT HAVE BEEN MOVED BY A WORD THAT YOU SPOKE, A SONG THAT YOU SUNG OR A MOMENT THAT YOU CAPTURED.

TO ALL WHO DON'T UNDERSTAND, WHO JUST CAN'T COMPREHEND AND WHO WANT YOU TO GET ON WITH IT FOR FEAR THAT YOU MIGHT BE THE NEXT ONE TO ASK THEM FOR SOME MONEY TO HOLD YOU OVER... GIVE THEM THE FINGER!!!! THE FREEDOM OF THE TONGUE MUST MATCH THE FREEDOM OF MY MIND!

 SO DON'T REVOKE MY GOD-CARD, FOR HE IS THE CREATOR AND I AM FROM HIM, THAT IS WHY I CREATE.

TO ARTISTS EVERYWHERE I COMMAND YOU TO LIVE ON, BREATHE ON, MOVE ON AND CREATE!

LEAVE THIS PLANET WITH A DONATION OF SOMETHING THAT CAN BE SEEN, HEARD OR SIMPLY REMEMBERED.

AND ON THE DAY OF YOUR GRAND FINALE WHEN YOU BID YOUR EARTHLY SUBJECTS ADIEU, LET ANOTHER PARAGRAPH BE ADDED TO YOUR OBITUARY WHILE YOUR MOURNERS ETERNALLY CRAVE A NEW SONG THAT YOU WON'T SING, A NEW NOTE THAT YOU WON'T PLAY, A NEW NOVEL THAT YOU WON'T WRITE, A NEW CANVAS THAT YOU'LL NEVER STROKE, A NEW VERSE THAT YOU'LL NEVER SPEAK FOR YOUR ENCORE PERFORMANCE WILL ONLY BE WITNESSED BY THE ARTISTIC DIRECTOR OF ALL CREATION.

UNTIL THAT DAY LET THE ARTIST LIVE AND FEAST ON ORGANIC CREATIVITY GIVING ARTISTIC BALANCE TO THE SCIENTIFIC, MOTION TO THE MUNDANE AND DEFINITION TO THE INEXPLICABLE!! HERE'S TO THE ARTIST!

OLD FOLKS, TIME ZONES AND PHONE NUMBERS

sfx: telephone rings

(groggy) Hello? Oh hi grandma, how are you? Good, that 's good. Grandma it's six o'clock in the morning. I said it's six o'clock in the morning Grandma! No Grandma I'm not yelling, I thought you couldn't hear me. I SAID I THOUGHT YOU COULDN'T HEAR ME! Oh so you can hear me now? No I didn't say that you wear me down. Turn the phone up Grandma, turn the phone up. Is it up now? Good. Grandma I love you and I'm always glad to hear from you but it's six o'clock in the morning. Yes, yes it's only six a.m. here. Yes I know it's nine o'clock there, it's always nine o'clock there when it's six o'clock here. Yes Grandma it's a three hour time difference, remember? Yes that's right it's only six o'clock here.

No I'm not up getting ready for work. I don't have to be at work until nine a.m. Since when? Well only since I moved here Ten Years Ago! I'm sorry I don't mean to yell it's just that I'm a little punchy at SIX in the morning. Oh don't cry Grandma, I hate it when you cry. I know that you've been up for hours and that you even waited a while before calling me but Grandma it's three hours difference in our time zones, three hours Grandma. Oh you KNOW it's three hours difference? You just forget weather it's three hours ahead or behind. Okay Grandma, okay. No I don't have company. No you're not disturbing me. It's just me and the cat. Did I hear what? No mother didn't tell me that Mrs. Sugarman had gall stones. What? Oh that's terrible. I'm sorry to hear that they had to cut off one of Old Man Peterson's toes.

It's so early Granny and I'm still not quite awake. Say what? You want to call me later when I'm awake? That'll be great. You say you want to call me at work? Okay, I guess that'll be all right. Here's the number. What? Okay I'll wait til you get a pen. (beat) You there Grandma? Okay, the number is three, two, three. What? Oh, okay that pen doesn't write. Okay. No I'll wait Grandma, no problem. (beat) Okay you ready? Okay! Three, two... what? Oh you have to turn the light on. Okaaay. Is it on? Good. Three, two, three, seven... huh? Slow down? Okay I'll slow down. Three, two, three, seven, nine. What? What is it now Grandma? Oh, you have to get your glasses. No, it's fine. I'm waiting, no problem. No problem. Okay, now where were we? Yes that's right. Three, two, three. No not seven five Grandma, seven, NINE. Seven, NINE. Huh? No, No. Not three, two ,three, seven, nine, seven, nine. I was telling you that it's seven nine INSTEAD of seven FIVE that's all. Okay let's start again my work number is three, two, three, seven, nine, four, that's right. Six, six, one... what? You say that's your other line ringing and you're going to click over? Noooo Grandma I just have one more digit to tell you and (abruptly) hello? Hello? Okay I'll just hold on for a few seconds and maybe she'll click back over and I won't get a.......... DIAL TONE!!! AGHHHH!!!!!!!

MASTER OF THE GREENS

In the quiet of the morning before anyone arrives

He gives the call to nature and beckons the sunrise

He's on post before the caddies or movement of the carts

He paints each placid fairway a tremendous work of art

He's the champion of champions, the commander of all unseen

He's the great score keeper, The Master of the Greens

So before each stroke of genius, before each focused swing

Give reverence to the sovereign Master of the Greens

Be not blind by competition nor flustered by the craft

Pay homage to the moment you stand en garde with shaft

Far greater than any handicap,

Or miraculous sweep from the dunes

Is the awesome pleasure

To feel such sweet commune

Let your mind go with wonder, let all praises flow

Let all questions now be uttered, seek all you want to know

For the course is His great classroom

Where the inquisitors convene

To absorb the mighty wisdom of

The Master of the Greens.

HE'S GONE (UNCLE BILLS POEM)

How empty is the feeling
How painful is every breath
How numb is each sensation
He's gone

What a gentle giant
What a strong and quiet force
What a sacrificing spirit
But he's gone

Never asking always giving
Always ready at beck and call
Never complaining, always willing
But now he's gone

Though he sits on wings of angels
Though his soul now flies on high
Though he calls a new place home
From my world he's gone

Oh how wrong to want to keep him
When his time is so well done
When his earthly temple has faded
Still I cry because he's gone

Though I knew he would be leaving
And that he should sit and suffer no more
I thought the parting would be much easier
But still he's gone

So say good-bye to my mighty soldier
Say good-bye to my long time friend
Good-bye my secret hero
I pray that I'll see him again
Now that he's gone

INNOCENT BYSTANDER

Would you aim your weapon with an innocent bystander standing by?
If you saw your enemy and felt enough malice in your heart to fire upon the person
that had inflicted harm upon you, would you fire upon him with an innocent bystander standing by?

If you were not certain that the bullets intended would only be sprayed upon your intended target,
would you still shoot?

Yet in the verbal weaponry of the domestic wars darts of steel are hurled without regard to the fact that fatal
phrases are falling like shrapnel upon vulnerable ears and impressionable minds without explanation or apology.

Young innocent bystanders are left with emotional scars, confused feelings, mixed messages
and all the residue of tempers out of control.
By merely being present they are living in the firing range.

Innocent bystanders, standing by, witnessing, guessing, feeling,
Innocent bystanders, standing by.

TIME

Time, time, constantly ticking, doing, fixing, mending, hoping, wishing, existing, racing time.

Time, time, pushing, rushing, fussing, cussing, shoving, stressing, time.

Time, calendars flipping, dates changing, schedules rearranging time.

Manipulating time, tripping over time, lamenting time, regretting time, fretting time.

Is anyone breathing, thinking, being, relaxing, remembering, resting, cherishing time?

BABY'S MAMAS/ DADDY'S DISDAIN

Man:	I hate that bitch, all she's about is manipulation and it ain't gonna work!
Woman:	He thinks that we need him and the fact is "we" don't. I'm just trying to keep my son from being another statistic that's all!
Man:	I buy him, everything he wants! Shoes, video games, whatever... all he has to do is name it! But I'm not giving up any cash so that she can spend it on herself!
Woman:	Where does he think that food comes from? Does he take for granted that I keep a roof over our heads? And what about all the times that I'm by my child's bedside in the middle of the night. Or riding the bus when my car isn't running to take him to school? I am there for my child and because of that he's got to pay.
Man:	It's always MY child this and MY child that! My, my, my! It's like I didn't have anything to do with it at all!
Woman:	He didn't even want the child and now he's professing to be the model parent. He's always frustrated and downgrading the child's mother, who happens to be me... and he wonders why we never had a chance at being a real family!
Man:	My family is my son! I owe nothing else to anybody in this world!
Woman:	My family is my child and he needs more than a weekend round of basketball.
Man:	He's gonna want his father some day! He's gonna come looking for me!
Woman:	The only reason my son will ever go looking for his father, is because his father wasn't there in the first place.
(beat)	
Woman:	I need thirty more dollars a month!
Man:	I ain't giving her shit!
BOTH:	I care for my child.
BOTH:	He's (she's) just my baby's mama (daddy).

CHURCH/ RELIGION/ SPIRITUALITY

Is the steeple, is it the people,
is it the practice or the principle?

What is it that aligns consciousness to a higher plane
what keeps this consciousness on a lower plane?

who agrees, who argues,
who accepts, who rejects

Is it only within your understanding?

your faith, your love, your source
your customs
your conditions

who are you believing
who are you reading
who are you following

what is merely tradition
what is fact
what is miracle
what is natural

who is God
what is God
what is?
what else matters
what?

REAL WEDDING VOWS (BRIDE)

*This piece can be performed by a single actor or actress or it can be performed as a scene by two or more players. It can also be broken into one or two separate monologues. One for the bride and one from the groom.

THE FLOWERS ARE IN BLOOM. THE PERFECTLY CARVED ICE STATUES SIT ERECT AND REGAL.

THERE ARE SHEETS OF DRAPED CHIFFON, RIBBONS AND BOWS THAT ADORN EVERY ARCH

AND ENTRANCE OF THE BANQUET HALL. THERE ARE FOUNTAINS FLOWING, HARPS ARE

PLAYING AND THE BIRDS ARE SINGING. YES, THIS IS HEAVEN AND THERE YOU ARE IN ALL

OF YOUR ANGELIC SPLENDOR GRACEFULLY APPROACHING THE THRONE OF MATRIMONY

CLAD IN EVERYTHING EXCEPT A PAIR OF GLASS SLIPPERS. BUT YOUR VISION IS CLOUDED

BY A SHRED OF FABRIC THAT COVERS YOUR COSMETICALLY ENHANCED FACE. THIS SHRED

IS OTHERWISE KNOWN AS A VEIL. THE REASON FOR THIS VEIL IS SYMBOLIC OF THE FACT

THAT YOU ARE BLIND. YOU ARE SO BLIND THAT YOU NEED SOMEONE TO HELP YOU DOWN

THE ISLE, PREFERABLY A BIG STRONG MAN THAT YOU'VE KNOWN SINCE CHILDHOOD.

STANDING AT THE GRAND PODIUM ARE THE GLEAMING ACCOMPLICES. THEY ARE

DRESSED IN SOME GOD AWFUL FROCK THAT PROBABLY ONLY FITS TWO OUT OF THE TEN OF

THEM BUT FOR THE SAKE OF SISTERLY LOVE, THEY ARE WEARING IT ANYWAY. THESE ARE

THE MEMBERS OF THE ROYAL COURT OF THE IMPENDING MATRIMONY. THEY ARE THE

FAITHFUL BRIDES MAIDS.

IF YOU'VE EVER WONDERED WHY THE BRIDE HAS SO MANY "MAIDS" AROUND HER,

IT'S BECAUSE SHE'S GOING TO NEED THEM; THE BRIDESMAIDS, THE MAID OF HONOR,

WHOEVER ELSE WILL ASSIST HER AS SHE ENTERS THE DOMESTIC DOLDRUMS KNOWN AS

MARRIED LIFE. INDEED SHE'S GONNA NEED A MAID AFTER THE MEETING OF ESTROGEN

AND TESTOSTERONE ATTEMPT TO OCCUPY THE SAME ABODE WITH A LEGAL SEAL THAT'S

SOMEWHAT SHORT OF A BLOOD COVENANT. AND NOW THE TIME COMES TO RECITE THE

NEW MARRIAGE VOWS. THE ECUMENICAL MUTTERINGS OF THE PAST HAVE BEEN REPLACED

BY WORDS THAT TRULY REFLECT THE LIFE OF BLISS THAT THIS MODERN DAY BRIDE IS ABOUT

TO ENTER. AND NOW, MAY WE ALL RISE FOR THE CEREMONY.

DEARLY BELOVED

WE ARE GATHERED HERE HOPEFULLY IN THE PRESENCE OF GOD AND ALL OF THESE PEOPLE

LISTED IN THEIR PERSONAL PHONE BOOKS TO JOIN THESE LIVES TOGETHER FOR AS LONG

AS POSSIBLE. BRIDE REPEAT AFTER ME.

(BRIDE)

I DO SOLEMNLY SWEAR TO TAKE THIS MAN

TO HAVE AND TO FOLD... HIS SHORTS, HIS SHIRTS AND WHATEVER ELSE HE LEAVES LYING

AROUND. I HEREBY PROMISE TO LOVINGLY ACCEPT HIS DROOL ON OUR DECORATIVE

PILLOWS EVEN THOUGH DECORATIVE PILLOWS ARE FOR DECORATIONS AND NOT FOR NAPPING

ON THE SOFA. I PROMISE TO CHECK THE GUEST BATHROOM IF MY HUSBAND WAS THE LAST

ONE TO USE IT.   I PROMISE TO CHECK THE REFRIGERATOR AND THE CABINETS FOR EMPTY

CARTONS AND CONTAINERS BEFORE GOING TO THE GROCERY STORE. I PROMISE THAT

AFTER MY FOURTEEN HOUR DAYS I WILL SAVE ENOUGH ENERGY TO MAKE

LOVE FEVERISHLY LIKE SOMETHING SHORT OF AN X RATED FILM.

I PROMISE TO PRETEND THAT HIS LOVE MACHINE IS THE BIGGEST ONE THAT I'VE EVER SEEN

IN MY LIFE BUT I WILL NOT LIE AND SAY THAT IT'S THE FIRST ONE I'VE SEEN, UNLESS OF

COURSE THAT IS THE TRUTH.

I DO SOLEMNLY SWEAR TO DISOWN ANY BRILLIANT PLANS AND LET HIM THINK

THAT IT'S HIS IDEA.

MAY WE LIVE HAPPILY EVER AFTER UNTIL DEATH, SNORING, LOVE HANDLES OR MY

MOTHER US DO PART.

NOW LET US PREPARE FOR THE ARRIVAL OF THE GROOM.

REAL WEDDING VOWS (GROOM)

LIKE A ZOMBIE HE HAS AGREED TO FABRIC SWATCHES, FLORAL PATTERNS AND MENU

ITEMS THAT ARE MEANINGLESS TO A GUY WHO JUST WANTS A GOOD FOOTBALL GAME,

A FEW HOT DOGS AND A SIX PACK BUT THIS WILLING GROOM HAS GONE ALONG WITH

THE PROGRAM SO FAR. ALL OF HIS RELATIVES ARE SETTLED IN FOR THE CEREMONY

AND HIS FIVE BEST FRIENDS ALONG WITH TWO OF HIS BROTHERS ARE PERCHED BESIDE

HIM IN STARCHED TUXEDOS LIKE A MILITARY COLOR GUARD. LORD KNOWS THIS IS

THE LAST TIME HE'S GONNA SEE HIS BOYS FOR A LONG TIME. STILL THIS LOVE SICK

LAD IS HYPNOTIC WITH ANTICIPATION FOR A LIFE LONG RENDEZVOUS WITH THE GIRL

OF HIS DREAMS. ALL THAT THIS EAGER GROOM REALLY WANTED WAS TO EAT A GOOD

MEAL AND GET LAID REGULARLY. A LIVE IN PARTNER IS MUCH MORE CONVENIENT AND

LESS COSTLY THAN ALL THOSE FRIDAY AND SATURDAY EVENING DATES, AND HIS MOTHER

IS MORE APPROVING OF A ROOM MATE WITH HER SON'S LAST NAME. OUR LOVING GROOM IS

ALSO LOOKING TO BE RELIEVED OF THOSE BURNT TV DINNERS AND CUPS OF NOODLES THAT

HE'S BEEN CALLING DINNER FOR THE PAST SEVEN YEARS. BUT AH YES, THIS UNION IS ABOUT

LOVE ISN'T IT. SO LET US PROCEED WITH VOWS FROM THE GROOM.

DEARLY BELOVED,

WE ARE GATHERED HERE IN THE SIGHT OF ALL OF THESE PEOPLE THAT

I DON'T EVEN KNOW, TO SAY GOOD-BYE TO MY SINGLE DAYS.

I DO SOLEMNLY SWEAR NEVER TO CLEAN UP THE BATHROOM AGAIN.

I SWEAR TO SPEND HUGE SUMS OF MONEY ON MECHANICAL JUNK THAT

I'LL ONLY USE ONCE AND THEN STORE IT IN THE GARAGE. I PROMISE TO BE HORNY

EVERY NIGHT AND EVERY MORNING. I PROMISE TO RAISE HELL AND MAKE HER WISH

SHE'D NEVER MARRIED ME AT LEAST ONCE A YEAR. I PROMISE TO PRETEND TO ENJOY

FISH STICKS AND STORE BOUGHT POTATO SALAD WHEN MY WIFE DOESN'T COOK

FROM SCRATCH.

I PROMISE TO TOTALLY FORGET WHY THERE'S A SINK IN THE KITCHEN IN THE FIRST PLACE.

I PROMISE TO EITHER BE TOTALLY IRRESPONSIBLE OR A COMPLETE MISER WHEN

IT COMES TO OUR MONEY.

I PROMISE TO ACT DUMBFOUNDED AS TO WHY MY WIFE DOESN'T LIKE MY

EX-GIRLFRIEND... THE ONE WHO STILL CALLS TO SAY HI. I PROMISE NEVER TO SAY

TO MY WIFE 'WELL YOU'RE NO SPRING CHICKEN EITHER.' I PROMISE NOT TO EVEN

NOTICE THE HOT SEXY OUTFITS THAT TONI BRAXTON AND JENNIFER LOPEZ WEAR

TO THE AWARD SHOWS. I PROMISE NOT TO LIKE HER NOSY GIRLFRIENDS WHO KNOW

ALL OF OUR BUSINESS. I PROMISE TO BE A ZOMBIE DURING SUPERBOWL SEASON.

I PROMISE TO REMEMBER ALL OF THE NBA STATS AND FORGET OUR ANNIVERSARY.

I PROMISE NOT TO LET THE STORE CLERK PICK MY WIFE'S CHRISTMAS PRESENT.

I PROMISE THAT NO MATTER HOW POOR WE ARE AS A COUPLE, I'LL ALWAYS

ORDER THE FIGHT ON PAY PER VIEW AND EXPECT MY WIFE TO MAKE SNACKS.

AND I ALSO PROMISE THAT AFTER OUR FAMILY TREE IS FULL , I'LL EITHER COME

HOME WITH A DOG OR A BRAND NEW SPORTS CAR.

FEEDING THE BEAST

IT'S THAT CRAVING, THAT LONGING, THAT BANGING ON THE CAGE,
THAT SOMETIMES RAGE THAT PROCLAIMS, THAT REQUESTS, THAT DEMANDS
TO BE FED. MANY TIMES IT IS MY FRIEND, SOMETIMES I AM SLAVE TO IT,
IT WAKES ME IN THE NIGHT, SOMETIMES CRADLES, SOMETIMES SHAKES ME IN THE
NIGHT, THE BEAST THAT MUST BE FED.

IT'S THE NAME I GIVE TO IT, THE TITLE, THE MARKER , THE MONIKER,
THE CREATIVE BEAST THAT SEES LANDSCAPES WHEN THERE IS NO CANVAS,
THAT HEARS MUSIC WHEN THERE'S NO SOUND, NO NOTES YET ON THE PAGE BUT
STILL THE SONG STIRS. THE CREATIVE BEAST THAT FINE TUNES EVERY
CHOREOGRAPHIC MOVE, WITH EYES SHUT AND TUNES IMAGINED.
THE CREATIVE BEAST THAT LAYS THE STORY FRAME BY FRAME.
THE CREATIVE BEAST THAT MUST BE FED; THAT CANNOT BE IGNORED.
THE BEAST THAT WILL PULL YOU BACK, DRAW YOU
BACK, DRAG YOU BACK TO DEFY THE COMPLACENT REALITIES. THE BEAST THAT IS
ONLY HARMFUL TO THE STATUS QUO. THAT BEAST THAT DEMANDS TO CREATE,
TO DRAFT, TO DRAW, TO PAINT, TO SING, TO DANCE, TO ACT, TO PLAY, TO SCULPT,
TO MOLD. TO BECOME ONE WITH THE CREATOR AND GIVE BREATH TO CREATIVITY
BY LETTING HIS HANDS BE YOUR HANDS, BY LETTING HIS VOICE BE YOUR VOICE,
BY LETTING HIS BODY BE YOUR BODY, BY BECOMING ONE WITH THE GREAT I AM
AND DISPLAYING WHAT YOU CAN NEVER EXPLAIN BUT BY ONE WORD AND THAT
WORD IS DIVINE.

THE GNAWING, THE URGE, THE DESIRE AND THE DUTY TO FEED THE BEAST,
THAT FEELING THAT THIS IS BIGGER THAN YOU, THE FEELING THAT WOULD HAVE
YOU QUIT IF YOU COULD, BUT YOU CAN'T FOR THE BEAST IS CONTROLLING,
MANIPULATING AND DAMN RIGHT STUBBORN, THE BEAST MUST BE FED ALWAYS.
THE CREATIVE BEAST MUST BE FED.

THE SINGING POET

THE SINGING POET IS ONE WHO SINGS AND RHYMES
WORDS RING AND MELODIES CHIME
BUT THERE WITHIN THE RHYTHM
THE POET CRAVES MORE THAN SONGS
AND THE SINGER NEEDS MORE THAN VERSE
TO EXPLAIN WHAT CANNOT BE CONTAINED
IN PHRASES SPOKEN OR SUNG

THE SINGING POET
CATCHES FRANTIC BREATHS OF REASON
SUBTLE SIPS OF PASSION
GLIMPSES AND QUICK GLANCES OF WORLDLY UNDERSTANDING
AND MERE TRACES OF AUDIBLE SOUND
THAT TINGLES THE DEPTH OF SOUL
WITHIN THE REALM THAT CAN NEVER BE UTTERED
BUT ONLY FELT, ONLY SILENTLY KNOWN

THE SINGING POET
IS RELUCTANTLY BOUND BY DEFINITION
BUT FAR TOO DEEP FOR WORDS
FAR TOO INTENSE FOR TONE
THE SINGING POET IS OFF THE SCALE
AND OFF THE PAGE
AND INTO THE STRATOSPHERE
WHERE THERE IS NO FEAR
THERE IS ONLY OMNISCIENT LIGHT
THAT BEGS TO TAKE FORM IN THE NOTION
AND IN THE MOTION OF THE SINGING POET

REMNANTS OF THE TIMES

Mature woman:	Where is that young black man who will be that old black man who is faithful to his old black woman and has been for fifty years?
Young woman:	Big mama, do you hear me? Did you hear what I just said?
Mature woman:	And where is that young black woman who would rather die an old black woman than live frivolously with just any man?
Young woman:	Big mama I appreciate your poetic analogies and ancient wisdom but I just poured my heart out to you and I'm hurting right now because I don't know what to do.
Mature woman:	Leave him alone, child.
Young woman:	But I love him.
Mature woman:	Leave him alone.
Young woman:	But I need him.
Mature woman:	Leave him alone.
Young woman:	But I...
Mature woman:	Leave him alone! He's married but not to you.
Young woman:	But mama
Mature woman:	Where is that young black man who will be that old black man who is faithful to his woman and has been for fifty years? Where is the young black man who is a young man like my father and my grandfather who put his wife and his family only second to God. Where are the providers who preside over their homes in love, peace, respect and authority. Where are these young men who will turn down a thousand women because they've committed to one and where are the young women who will say no thanks and so long? Where are they? Do they exist or are they just remnants of the times? (She turns to the young woman) Leave him alone!

PEOPLE WHO DON'T KNOW

This is an open letter to all the people who don't know. This is to people who don't know that your breath stinks. Dear stinky breath people, if everyone seems to be backing away from you when you talk and it's not because you're holding a hand grenade, then there's good chance that your breath spells like a portable toilet by a construction site. It's time to buy a vowel and solve the puzzle, you're breath is cooking like a pot of chitterlings on a hot summer day.

This is an open letter today to all the people who don't know. There's also a message for people who don't know that their children are unattractive. Dear people who don't know that your children are unattractive. We don't want to see their baby pictures, we don't want to know how many people have told them that they look like super models and it doesn't matter if they ever get their braces taken off, they're just not cute kids.

Dear People who don't know that you can't sing. If you're turned down to perform at Karaoke Bars even though you've met the five drink minimum there's something wrong. If you can't even get booked to sing at a church basement wedding then you really can't sing. If the senior citizens are saying that they'd rather just drool and talk to themselves, then there's a good chance that you really can't sing.

Then there's the people who can't cook. These are the folks who will serve no food until it's burnt. Dear people who don't know that you can't cook, if your dinner is not ready until the fire department shows up, you can't cook. If your hot dogs are not done until they look like Vienna sausages then you can't cook. If your rice is not done until it's crunchy and black, give it up, you can't cook.

There are also a great deal of people who don't' know that they're crazy! These are usually the people who show up in your family tree. They may not be clinical but they always have a crisis that involves you making a trip to Western Union or eventually a sleeping arrangement that most likely involves your couch or extra bedroom. These relatives are also expert psychologists when it comes to examining everyone else's life although their life would be a case study.

Dear Lazy folks. You know you're lazy don't you? Why else would you have so much time on your hands? You haven't been to med. school. You didn't invent Microsoft but you've got more leisure time than the Sultan of Brunei. You're lazy.

Dear people who don't know that no one wants your advice, how can I say this, we don't want your advice so shut up.

I am closing my letter to all the dear people for they now know that enough is enough. I expect a change in your behavior. Should I get a letter from you in the near future I must inform you that I will not read it. I'm far too narrow minded to take a look at myself.

I LEFT BEFORE I LEFT

I parted you know. Long before I packed my bags or changed my address, I left. I left before I left. I hadn't been there for a while. After I was shut out emotionally, kept distant physically and detached spiritually from this situation, after trying desperately to make contact with a closed consciousness, I felt it necessary to leave. After my pleas were met with anger, my longings for two way conversation were met with a that's final and a walk away, a *walk away* became inevitable for me.

Somewhere between my last attempt at communication and pure honest connection I left. Somewhere after such confident misunderstanding and misinterpretation of the person *I am*, the person *I was*, the *person I am trying to be,* I made a decision that if you're addicted to conflict then there is no addiction to me. I'm addicted to be free, as in free to be, free to be the loving me and to have that love reciprocated in a healthy manner. If the previous attempts at loving me are the examples of what it's like to be loved by you then let me love myself from now on and since I'm loving myself, by myself. And since I've already left in a mental and spiritual kind of way, then the rest of me might as well leave too. Yes I left, not due to any other person, not due to any lack of love but thanks to *you* I left, thanks to *me*, I left. Thanks. I left and *I left* before I left.

ON THE DANCE FLOOR

Has it ever happened to you? You casually accept an invitation to the dance floor, cop a confident stroll and commence to getting your groove on to your favorite song and then you discover that your partner is on a mission to be the wildest, maddest, ecstatic body in the room. It's like flashbacks of Saturday Night Fever, Footloose, Breakin or some Fred Astaire and Ginger Rodgers movie except *those* people could dance but what you're seeing here is like some crazy coed on an acid trip or heaven forbid having an unknown seizure or just a really bad itch happening all over his/her body. You move, you try to be smooth, cool, play if off like you can be poised enough for the both of you but this baby is going for broke and cranking it up by the notches with each pulsating beat of the blasting music from the high tech state of the art PA system. Then suddenly you notice that everyone else has left the dance floor, they've given up and surrendered the moment to you and Rene the Rhythm-less wonder.

The music is pounding, pounding and your partner is spinning and spinning, gyrating, jumping, kicking, twirling, bending, gagging, smiling and clicking and not one motion has been in synch with the song that the DJ is currently playing. And you think, Lord why me? Why didn't I see this freak of nature coming? Why didn't the rabbit coat and platform shoes alert me that I was in for a date with dancing death? Meanwhile, the grim reaper is getting his/her groove on and you're wishing you could dig a hole and crawl six feet under the dance floor of doom. Suddenly the music stops and you run for cover leaving your partner breathless like a puppy that's just chased a Frisbee along the foggy coast of the Pacific Ocean. As you slip out of the back door breathless and embarrassed you vow never ever to dance again as long as there's four beats to a measure and am empty seat at the bar!

DATE RACE (outside only)

I want to share something with you. It's kind of personal and I hope that you won't judge me for it. (BEAT) While I think you are a very nice person... and you seem to have a lot going for yourself, uhm I just don't date anyone that is my same race. I have found that the available significant others within my race are too complicated, boring and ignorant to be exact. So basically I've made a decision to see color... that is, I made a decision to see every color but my own when making a choice about my romantic interests.   I felt a bit strange at first and believe me I was criticized quite heavily. One person even went as far as to call me a sick bastard who denied my very own culture and I thought, now see that's why I don't date your type anymore. I tell you it is easier for me to just ignore the whole race than to take a chance on getting any more of the bull that I've been getting all in the name of keepin' it real! A real mate doesn't judge me all the time, a real mate doesn't have an attitude all the time, a real mate isn't always jealous or mad at the whole damn world! A real mate isn't so psychologically damaged that they see everything as black or white. A real mate isn't always challenging me! Sometimes I'm responsible, sometimes I'm not.   Sometimes I'm sensitive, sometimes I'm not. Sometimes I'm wonderful, sometimes I'm not!   So if I have to date outside my race just to get some peace from a place that is not so convoluted then that's what I'll do!! (beat) I told my mother about this decision and it hurt her very deeply.   She asked me if my decision actually made me a racist.
I said; 'I don't know Mom, does it?'

DATE RACE (outside response)

I thought that this was the most wonderful person that I had ever met. This was a person that was intelligent, strong, sexy, funny, caring and very available. We were from the same home town and the same religious background. We had similar professional interests and we just hit it off in every way. We had so much fun together. I looked forward to our weekly encounters at the local coffee shop. Still no one had broken the ice to get a phone number or book a date. So I'm thinking what is the problem? The next time we meet I'm going for it! I mean the chemistry that we had was off the Richter scale. Why not take it to the next level? Well the day came and as usual we engaged in our charming impromptu conversations. This was the kind of person that made you tingle on the inside. Today I was not letting the moment slip away. I waited for a few seconds to see if things were going to end in the usual 'see ya' later' fashion and it seemed as if they were. So I took deep breath, paused a moment and went for it! 'Hey before we just run off, how about exchanging phone numbers so that we can get together for a date.' (long beat) I can't believe what happened next. It was like a throw back to the Civil Rights era except that this didn't happen thirty years ago, this happened yesterday. This beautiful person whose skin has the same tone as mine told me that he/she didn't date within his/her own race anymore. This brilliant person had somehow measured all of his/her past experiences and equated them to discount his/her entire race for any credible prospects for intimate relationships. So from now on anyone who bore the same skin tone and ethnic background was automatically excluded. I must admit that I felt bad for a moment, then I realized that I wasn't missing out on anything. They say love is blind but this was a kind of blindness that I didn't care to even try to understand.

DATE RACE (inside only)

I love what I love and I'm not ashamed to tell you that there is nothing on this earth like my beautiful black queen/king. I love the strength, I love the rhythm, I love the passion, I love the fury, I love the music, I love the black!   I love the hair, I love the straight, I love the kinky, I love the curly, I love the dreads, I love the twists, I love the corn rows, I even love the finger waves! I just love it black like that! I love everything from corporate to ghetto, from classical to hip hop. I love the flavor! I love the milk chocolate, the dark chocolate, the mocha and the cafe au lait. I love the honey brown and the tragic mulatto. I love the politics! I love the revolution! I love the food! From the ribs to the tofu, weather it's a meal with your pinkie out or a supper where you sop til the gravy don't stop. I just love the blackness! I love the language, I love everything from 'Why certainly my dear' to the 'Yea Mufuka' That sounds like a mufukinplan to me. I love the way we communicate. I love the code. I love the Whatz Zup, meet me at the crib and no CP time so give me a holler cause I'm Audi 5 now peace out to the H-N-I-C!   For me It's more than color, it's about culture and I love the culture. I love the understanding of who I am because that's who you are so we're cool like 'dat! Cool like Martin and Coretta, Ozzie and Ruby, Denzil and Paula, Mack 10 and T-Boz, Holly and Rod. It's ebony cool like Lamont and Peaches, Greg and Andrea, Paul and Renee, Musa and Vida, Mary and Bill, Delores and Columbus and all the rest.   It's black on black love and it's all to the good! I love it all y'all!

DATE RACE (Inside response)

Now this was the type of intriguing person that I would love to get to know better. In fact I found it rather challenging to understand the inner complexities of this dynamic individual. Yes I was definitely amused by this attractive specimen and I could tell that the feeling was somewhat mutual but I did feel a resistance towards us becoming closer. Despite my subtle hints, we never made any plans for any future dates or conversations. I turned up the charm and the sex appeal but to no avail. I did everything that fell within sophisticated reasoning to let this person know that I was interested and available but I got no response. Finally I asked, 'Is it my gender?' and he/she said no that's not it. So then I asked: 'Is it my race?' and he/she said yes. 'Yes, you are a nice person but I don't date outside my race.' That's what he/she said. That's what I heard. I admit, I kind of had a feeling that this was the reason for the hesitation but having it confirmed brought me face to face with my own humanity. I had felt discrimination. Should I work harder to prove to this person that I was a loving and caring individual who didn't see color. Should I tell him/her that I meant no disrespect to all of the men/women in his/her own race. Should I also tell him/her that my family insisted that we love and respect everyone the same. Should I set out on a mission to let him/her know how different I was or should I let it go? And then I was ashamed by my next set of thoughts. Even if this person accepted me, could I possibly understand a world in which I had never lived? And what about the children? Would they be looked at as beautiful and given special privileges due to their exotic appearance? Would I always feel that I was being compared to the other race of potential spouses that got left behind? Could I compete? Would I care? Would I somehow feel that I had gotten a coveted prize? He/she said he/she wished to be no more than friends, just friends and for the first time in my life I wondered what it would be like to have different skin. If everything else were the same but only my skin were different would he/she want me then? If that were the case, would I still want to be wanted?

DATING (Neutral)

Dating, dating, dating! What is the obsession? Black, white, brown, yellow... whatever! Look from now on I have just one criteria.... NO MORE FOOLS! I don't care what color they are!   I'm not paying any one else's bills, fixing their problems, solving their childhood issues or pretending that I like their parents or their pets.   I'm way past the race issue. I'm just looking for a great person but hey I still got my prejudices. I'm not particularity into dating anyone that's heavier than I am or anyone who has more kids than I do.   Short has never been a turn on unless they're short with money. Bad breath and raggedy shoes are always out with me and I'm big on the religion issue. I mean sometimes I mix my meats and carbohydrates, I like presents for Christmas, and I just believe that a good Italian Hot link sausage should be made out of pork. Okay I can compromise on the pork but I don't want candles and incense burning in my house all the time, I've got allergies!

Okay, I don't know if it's politically correct to be prejudiced about the things that I just mentioned but if you know anyone who meets my criteria and they're available, give me a call so that I can interview them for myself.   Oh and by the way, if it's a serious love connection that ends up in matrimony then I'll invite you to the wedding. I didn't say you could be in the wedding, I said I'd invite you and don't forget to bring a nice gift after all I like presents!

For Women

THIS YEAR I'M JUST GON' BE ME

This year I'm just gon' be me!   That's right I'm just gon' take a year off from solving all of the problems of all of civilization... and be me! Now I know how long we've suffered and struggled to build this nation and I know that that there is still much work to be done, but for once, for a change, I'm just gon' be a normal person with a normal life. Just this once, I'm gon' take a year off from watching PBS and I'm gon' check out the movie channel, that's right the *American* Movie Channel.

This year when I run into one of those long lost relatives with one of those sad, sad stories; well, right before they get to the part about *'Can they and their six kids come live with me,* I'm gon' grab em by the hand, sweetly look them in the eye and say: Child, good luck" and be on my way.

This year I'm just gon' be me. When I don't feel like it, I'm gon' say: *"I Don't Feel Like It!"* And let me tell you another thing, this year I ain't buying no candy from those children in the grocery store parking lot.   When they come up to me with those big puppy dog eyes asking: 'Would you like to buy some candy?'   I'm gon' say: "NO!! I'm saving up for a pedicure, now go home!"

This year, I'm just gon' be me. I'm not going to explain myself to anyone. I'm not going to break it down to anyone who doesn't understand why a woman living in these changing times might become so fatigued that she would even need or deserve a three hundred and sixty five day *H I A T U S* (that means *rest*, for those of you who went to a community college)!

This year when a girlfriend that I haven't heard from in a long time calls me and says: 'Hey girl, whatcha doin?'   I'm going to put down that TV remote so I can put my other hand on my hip and say: "What have I been doin?....*nothing!"*

I AM AFRICAN AMERICAN

I AM AFRICAN AMERICAN

BUT HEY, DON'T LET MY CHEMICALLY TREATED TRESSES FOOL YOU

EVERY SIX WEEKS, I GO BACK TO MY ROOTS

SO I KNOW WHO I AM AND I KNOW WHERE I'M FROM

I AM AFRICAN AMERICAN

BUT HEY DON'T LET THE NICE NEW CAR FOOL YOU,

MY GREAT, GREAT GRAND DADDY DIDN'T HAVE ANY SHOES

AND HE HAD TO WALK TWENTY FIVE MILES TO SCHOOL.

I AM AFRICAN AMERICAN

BUT HEY, DON'T LET THE MANICURE FOOL YOU

I STILL KNOW HOW TO PICK SOME GREENS AND STRING SOME BEANS

AND DO ALL THOSE OTHER ETHNIC THINGS.

I AM AFRICAN AMERICAN

BUT HEY DON'T LET THE GRAMMAR FOOL YOU

CAUSE I STILL KNOW HOW TO *GO THERE*

WHEN IT'S NECESSARY TO *GO THERE*.

I AM AFRICAN AMERICAN

BASEBALL, HOT DOGS AND BLACK EYED PEAS.

WHAT YOU SEE

A piece for one or more actors dressed in various styles of night clothes, PJ's, sweat suits or T-shirts, head scarves, doo rags, etc.

(BKG. MUSIC THE DRAMATICS, WHATCHA SEE IS WHATCHA GET)

Good morning, good morning, good morning baby. Oh, I know you're kinda shocked. You're probably thinking, "Now I know that's not the same person I took to bed last night." But it's me baby and I'm all yours.

I thought about telling you that I was just a wee bit *unattractive* in the mornings but I figured you'd find out soon enough. You know what? I think people should walk around like this all time. It's so liberating.

You said you liked natural beauty, so here I am!!! (beat) What's wrong?
You look like something's wrong. What's the matter pookie! I'm still your little love dove.

What? You say I look like I had a rough night. No way, I slept like a baby! I dreamed I was the richest and happiest person in the world! This is just the way I look, everything else is just some clothes on a hanger and tonic in a bottle.

Think about it. All the people at your job look like me when they wake up, even that new cutie pie you had your eye on. In the morning time it's just scattered hair and buttermilk breath for all of mankind. Even the constitution says all men are created equal. That's what it means! We're just one family of ugly folks in the morning.

Now stop standing there with your face all wrinkled and come give me a kiss.
No, not on the cheek. Give me a big fat juicy one. What?! (beat)

WELL THAT'S NOT WHAT YOU SAID LAST NIGHT!

SATURDAY AT SEAN'S

It was Saturday at Sean's and I knew it was going to be a day long event. You see, Sean is the best weaver in town and all the divas come to him to get their *Doo* done! I mean Sean knows how to do those undetectable "Nu-ahn, girl I thought that was all your real hair" weaves. And that's exactly why I endure five or more hours of salon captivity on a weekly basis. This particular Saturday the shop was extra busy. When I got there he had already done three weaves, two perms and a press n' curl and it was just ten o'clock. Now all I needed was a re-touch and to have my tracks tightened before I went back in front of the cameras on Monday. My friend J.P. whose an up and coming comedian had also come to the shop and it was urgent that she see Sean because she had gotten a bad weave (somewhere else of course) and she still had glue stuck in her hair. J. P. travels a lot and she's the kind of sister who needs to have her hair swinging back and forth while she's working the crowd.   Then Marleen shows up with a head full of braids. She's a singer who was just coming off the road and she needed to get her hair done before the Soul Train Awards which was happening in a few days. So she sat down and proceeded to take down the first of her two hundred braids.

I finally got my old weave hair taken out and Sean suggested that I use another kind of hair this time so that it wouldn't get so tangled in between salon visits. Now conveniently enough, Sean's salon is located around the corner from Fake Hair Row, you know the street where you can get everything from toupees to false eye lashes. So I took off to get my new batch of 100% human hair. I asked if anybody else needed anything before I left. You know, perhaps someone needed a new ponytail, a fall, a bag of synthetic hair, or maybe even some ringlets but everyone was cool.   While taking my short walk, I kinda drifted for a moment and wondered why nobody ever gave those braided divas any grief. They've got two or three bags of store bought hair in their heads and it's synthetic! At least mine is real. How come weave divas get all the static? Well, In a few minutes I was back and the clients just kept on strolling in. Man I never saw so many divas showing up in hats and sun glasses. It looked more like a Dick Tracy audition. Meanwhile, Sean was fluffing 'em up and sending them on their way. Everything from bobs to boy cuts, he did with the greatest of ease.

By this time another well known singer and her daughter came in. He touched her up, and got her conditioner on and sat her under the diva's holding tank....the dryer! Some other lady came in and she kept bugging Sean to give her some streaks and he kept telling her no, she wasn't getting any streaks. If she asked him once, she asked him fifty times and he kept telling her; "No, not today!"

I had somehow gotten washed, conditioned and was being blown dry and it had only been four hours! Then the jewelry man came in. Since I was kinda stuck there I thought it was a good time to try on some of his toe rings. So now I'm thinking; "Boy, I sure hope nobody I know comes up in here and sees me with only half of my hair on with one shoe on and one shoe off trying on toe rings! I found a cute one and I bought it. By this time Marleen had managed to take down about twenty of those two hundred braids in her hair and I guess J.P. felt kinda sorry for her and started helping her. After I got my hair sown in I started helping her too.   And then He came in. He was tall and sorta walked with a limp but I could tell he was packing a lunch! For real!!! He was the bar-b-que man!! All you could hear all over the salon was: "Girl, where's my purse? Do you have change for a twenty? Do y'all got any rib tips."   It was like the dead coming back to life again. All you could see were diva's dipped over plastic containers licking and sucking the sauce off of their freshly painted fingers. And yes, the food was indeed good! I had the *beef* bar-b- que, if you must know. It was a very long day but at the end of it I looked marvelous. And in some small way, I celebrated being a black woman cause I knew that at Super Cuts and Fantastic Sam's, they just didn't have this much fun!

BUTTERFLIES AND TREES

Everybody always told me that I was going to be a *star*. Even my kindergarten teacher knew something was a little different about me after our first school play. You see, I wanted to be a butterfly because the butterflies were the *stars* of the show. They wore these beautiful pink costumes and they got to flutter all over the stage throughout the whole show. Well instead, I was told that I was going to play the part of a tree. And I thought; 'I don't wanna play no tree.' All the children playing trees had to wear these real ugly brown leotards with a brown cardboard tube over them and a head piece made out of green construction paper shaped like leaves. And all they had to do was poke their arms out and stand there. Besides there were so many trees, how would my mama know which one was me. I was so mad. Actually I was mad and sad at the same time. I cried and cried so hard that my mama had to go up to the school and talk to that lady. I mean, the nerve of her casting my mama's child in the part of a tree. Mama said she was probably partial to them doctors' and lawyers' kids. So she marched up to that school and talked to that teacher. But mama didn't do what I thought she was gonna do. I wanted her to talk to that teacher the way that she talked when she was mad at me. Instead, mama was all nice and polite. I couldn't believe her. I said to myself; "Dog, my mama done turned on me." Well anyway, I guess it was just too late to change the whole program around just because one person's vain child couldn't get over the fact that she was not STARRING in her first production at the age of five. The teacher explained that she didn't know it was so important to me and that she'd look out for me the next time. Once again I thought to myself, "What does she mean *next time?* How many times does she think I'm going to be in kinny garden?" I was real good in coloring and I had learned my ABC's so I knew that I was going to the first grade on time!! Finally the big day rolled around. Mama and all the other parents crowded into the auditorium. Then the music started and the big red velvet curtains opened. The moment had come, it was time for me to make my grand debut! I glided onto the stage, graceful and proud knowing that I was the best tree there ever was! (beat) I sure wish that teacher could see me now!

WHAT IS THAT I SMELL

What is that I smell? Is it you? Cause if it is, you sure do smell good!

What's the name of that? I gotta get some of that for my baaay-bee!

       What is that I smell? Now I know I cleaned out this refrigerator a couple of days ago.

       I wish I could find out what's causing that awful odor?! Maybe its the garbage disposal.

What's that I smell? Every time I come over to your house it always smells *so* nice.

Is it fresh flowers, is it potpourri or is it that new stuff you shake all over your carpet?

       What is that I smell? Oh I just hate coming to hospitals.

       It's sort of like a combination of sick folks and cleaning fluid.

What's that I smell? The scent grabbed me when I opened the front door.

Grandma, I can always tell when you're making something special.

       What is that I smell? I'm tired and I'm just getting home from work.

       I hope those kids remembered to cut my pot off at four thirty.

What is that I smell? Now you know some people don't believe in wearing deodorant.

But what I can't figure out is; "Why would she mess up a nice outfit like that?"

       What is that I smell? I finished my cycle last week!

       As much as I talk about everyone else, I just know it can't be me.

What is that I smell?

I'VE BEEN HURT BUT I'M NOT MORTALLY WOUNDED

I've been hurt, but I'm not mortally wounded. Yes, there have been many times when I've felt a pain so deep that I wanted to die. You name it, loneliness, depression, confusion, frustration, grief, I've experienced all of it. But I still want to live. I still know that there are good things in life that I will achieve. I'm achieving them right now! I am happy and I am peaceful because I have survived it all. Now some experiences took a little more time to work through but here I am and I feel terrific. Some people believe that God does bad things to people so that He can teach them something but I don't believe that anymore. I believe that I am a student of the universe and I came here to learn. I believe that God allows me and everyone else the room to make their own choices and learn life's lessons and that He is there to love us no matter what. I believe that He teaches us through His word, that's how He teaches. How could I love and trust someone who would deliberately hurt me in order to show me something. That doesn't fit my methodology.

Yes, I've been hurt. But I'm not mortally wounded because I want to go forward in life having benefited from those things in the past that have shaped me and made me the person that I am today. I want to keep on living and keep on loving over and over again. And you know what? I'm not mad at anybody. By releasing the hurt and the anger, I released all the pain. And I feel free! In fact some of the people who caused me the most pain have served as my greatest teachers! But so what? I forgave them all and my heart is unencumbered. While I don't have the answer to everything, I certainly don't let anybody walk all over me...*anymore*. Many things are beyond my control and beyond my own personal realm of reasoning. But I choose to live harmoniously in this universe. And I prayed for the peace that passes all understanding. I've learned to adopt a humble acceptance for all the things that I cannot change. I am energized to do that which I *can* do diligently and with love. I have learned to take care of me because I matter. I can give love and I can receive love but I must first love me!

SISTAHS GOT PHONES

Everywhere you go you'll see them popping up out of purses, back packs and glove compartments honey, sistahs got phones! I mean no matter where I am, at the mall, at the gym and even at the grocery store sistahs are all on the phone talkin' bout " meet me here" or "meet me there" or "look for me out front in about ten minutes." It is so simply elegant! From Wall Street to Compton sistahs got phones!!

When I first started dating I was always told to take enough money in case I needed to make a phone call. But now if a date gets out of hand all I have to do is slip to the restroom and press 911 send! If I'm out dining by the water front or the local burger shack and I happen to run into my best friend's boyfriend who is having dinner with "someone" he's not supposed to be with, I can prance over to that table, whip out my telephone, call my girlfriend and inform brother man that someone would like to speak to him!   Well, I wouldn't actually do that, but the thought sure is tempting. I'm wondering what did people do when they had to rush to a mere phone booth! It took me long enough to get used to the cordless phone and now this! I'm still getting over it!! Sistahs got phones!!!

SEXY IN A PANTSUIT

I found out! I can be sexy in a pantsuit. Now there was a time when I thought it was all about being all sucked in, tucked up and tantalizingly tight. But I found out that I can be sexy in a pantsuit! I don't have anything against pantyhose and high heeled pumps are just fine but who wants to be bothered with that all the time? I found out that I can work it just as well is a sassy, classy textured and tailored pantsuit! I've discovered a whole new dimension. I've learned the art of *mental* seduction. Gentleman of discriminating taste find that so intriguing. It's like they can't quite put their finger on it, they just know that there's something about you. Suddenly they notice my pretty brown eyes or the softness of my skin and don't let me have my hands and feet done when I'm wearing a chic pair of open toe shoes. It's all over! Now, I haven't thrown away all of my little black dresses or my red pumps either for that matter but I'm so glad that I've found out that I can be fiercely sexy in a pantsuit!

SHORT DRESSES IN CHURCH

She walked into the morning worship service in a gold micro-mini skirt with a long wig on and heavily applied make up.

Like clockwork you could see the sisters' heads turning and their eyes sizing her up. Big flowery hats began to bend one to another with murmurs of "Oh would you look at her" or "where did she come from" or any of the likely responses.

Their scorn was evident. Their un-acceptance was chilling and not in the least bit discrete despite their devout and holy posture. No one took a moment to remember the testimonies of all the things that they had done and of what God had delivered them from.

These are the same saints that proudly parade their modest attire shouting hallelujah, rejoicing and saying amen.

Who would talk to this stranger, who would welcome her in? Who would see past her attire and invite her back again?

QUIRKS

Quirks, we've all got 'em. Especially when it comes to men. Now personally I like a tall man or a short man who walks tall. But I can't stand a tall man who hunches over when he walks or a short man who has little bitty arms and when he reaches up to shake hands with you he kinda strains like his clothes shrunk in the wash or something.

Something else I look out for is good teeth. Now I know that not everyone is born with a perfect smile, and not everyone had the privilege of wearing braces but I at least expect to kiss a man with all of his teeth on the same row. And I don't mind if the brother is missing a few teeth here and there but just not right in the front. While we're on the subject, I don't have a problem with a man that brushes his teeth on a regular basis either. But I can't deal with a butter mouth. You know a Butter Mouth!...someone whose grins glistens like Land O' Lakes, as in Land O' Lakes butter. The thought of scraping a pound of butter off of someone's incisors before kissing them is rather nauseating. Which brings me to my next point. Bad breath. Has anyone ever tried to kiss you with bad breath? Have you ever accidentally breathed in while someone with bad breath was breathing out and it was almost like you swallowed the scent of the stench in their mouth? Have you ever offered a breath mint to someone and they thought that you were just being nice but you were really trying to help them tame that rancid odor that was parting their lips. This is disgusting. See I have figured out how to keep from kissing a person like this without hurting their feelings. Just tell them that you have a cold and if that doesn't work, tell them you have a big green fever blister on your tongue and if that doesn't work, tell them that you have mononucleosis. If the mononucleosis line doesn't work, tell them that you're a taste tester for a new brand of edible fertilizer.

Not many people know this but another major quirk among sophisticated singles and married folks alike is feet. Do you know how many guys I've met that are missing a toenail. Do you know that there are guys that actually wear corn pads? Do you also know how many guys there are that clip their toenails in the rug and never vacuum them up? Some of those old brown toenails are never found until Aunt Betty slips her fingers through the sofa cushions looking for loose change after Thanksgiving Dinner. Have you ever seen a well dressed good looking guy that was so handsome that he just took your breath away and then you saw him at the church picnic wearing sandals and his toes were crooked in about five different directions? Didn't it make you wonder why he would even wear sandals in the first place? What about folks with real crusty heels who always want to put their feet in your lap? And while we're on it what about the dudes with stinky feet? I mean the feet are just funky for no reason.

There are also those who prefer good shoe-sock coordination. That means if your suit is brown and your shoes are brown, then your socks ought to be....brown! Let's try another example. If your suit is green and your shoes and tie are black, then your socks ought to be either green or black not blue! Shoes needn't be expensive or brand new but a nice shine is a sign of a well groomed man.

Another annoyance is the man who doesn't know when to go home. If at the end of an evening no one has said anything for the last five minutes then Hey Fella!...get a clue, *go home!*

Now I know that looks are only skin deep and people are people but heed a word to the wise, these are things that we talk about on the phone with our girl friends...five minutes after the date is over and sometimes before you even get to your car...or in some cases, the bus stop. Quirks, we've all got 'em.

AIR FRESHENER

Dear Mr. Air Freshener Company,

This is an open letter to you. I am well aware that as human beings it is necessary that we "eliminate" on a regular basis and I am also aware that such "elimination" varies in its fragrant quotient depending on the occasion. I am so happy that your company has so crafted such a product that is designed to lend a bit of sweetness to such a private and unsavory moment. But I want to know is...what makes you think the smell of orchid peach, Dutch apple or rose goes with "elimination?!!" As a citizen and a consumer I am requesting that you develop something stronger. To me apples, roses and peaches are scents that are best suited in other parts of the house but certainly not in the little room at the end of the hall. There are people in my house that are no match for the floral fruity scented aerosol in the pink can. Shoot, I got a grandmother that can do man sized damage in that same little room. And sometimes, I think that some of what grandma leaves in that room had been inside her for the last eighty years. Why don't you give the people what they really need? Blowtorch baking soda, Poisonous Pine or Neutralizing Nitrate. That's what I need in a can of air freshener. Fruit belongs in the kitchen and flowers belong in the garden. Please tell your very trained scientists to go back to work. The latrine is a popular place around my house and well...we really need your help.

Yours Truly,

Betty Crock.
(or Glade In The Shade)

FELLOWSHIP

Sometimes I like kickin' it with my buddies. We don't have to do anything special or even go anywhere. I just like being with people that make me feel good. They don't sweat me and I don't sweat them. We just seem to flow with the moment, whatever the moment brings. We can go from discussing old boy friends to who caught the latest shoe sale quicker than you can say: "Girl, turn to channel five, there was an earthquake in Japan!" We encourage one another and we laugh at each other's jokes. And we endlessly listen to different stages of the same old story. But its cool because we're truly there for one another. Whether we're sipping cappuccino on the boulevard or pursuing the latest art display we're content just being buddies. We don't compete with each other and we certainly don't put each other down. Of course we don't see things exactly the same way all the time but we respect each other's right to be different. My buddies are all like different sides of me. As I get to know them, I get to know me. Me and my buddies, we got it goin' on.

ALL MY MAMAS

This is dedicated to all my mamas! Who says you only get one? I didn't! I got a whole lot of mamas and I love them all! An old African proverb says that it takes a village to raise a child and contrary to popular belief, it is not a saying that Hillary Clinton made up. Well God surely loves me because I got my whole village and then some! My first and most cherished Mama is of course the lady whose responsible for getting me here and her name is Florence. I always called her Ma Dear. She was the youngest and feistiest of nine children born to Walter Guy and Willie Gertrude Hawkins in Athens, Georgia but the family took pride in their big move to the North; Memphis, Tennessee. Mama Florence was a twin who was born fifteen minutes after her paternal twin Floretta. My mama was known for being sweet and having a pleasant sense of humor but she was not one to cross. She definitely knew how to stand up for herself. My mama wasn't scared of anybody. She was one proud lady. I was told that there wasn't a woman at Booker T. Washington High School that had prettier legs and a smaller waist than my mama. Florence took pride in being a drum major back in the time that those honors were only bestowed on high yellow girls or the children of under takers or physicians. But my mama's true talent was in music. She liked to play the piano. She even had a group back in the fifties called the Memphis Jubilees and they used to sing on the radio. I know this because one of my aunts gave me a newspaper clipping of my mama from back in the day, mama was so pretty. She looked like a brown skinned Dorothy Dandridge. Mama was also very independent. She always tried to make things better but I think that things would have been different if times hadn't been so hard when she was a girl. I remember coming home one day and I was crying because somebody at school had called me a black! Now I *was* black but at this time we were still Negroes so being called black wasn't a compliment. My mama told me the next time that happens to put my hands on my hips, stand up to that person and shout; "Say it loud, I'm black and I'm proud!" I'll always remember that!

I also didn't know that neither I nor my mother were expected to live after my birth. My head was resting on a tumor that my mother had and she was very ill. Well after she pulled through the birth, the doctor told her that he wasn't sure if I would make it. My mama told that doctor; "This child is going to live because God said so! And my mama was right cause here I am!! Now I didn't get to spend that much time with my mama but she always left me with the nicest people. That's how I met Mama Green.

Mama Green met me when I was just six months old in Nashville, where I was born. She started out being just a baby-sitter and ended up being one of my mamas! Mama Green is a fair skinned, heavy set woman that stands about four eleven. Now her grand father was a slave named Richard Jameson. I'm not talking about some woman who lived back in the 1800's, this woman is alive today. Well after her and Daddy Green's children were grown they started taking care of foster children. There was Jackie and Henry (who were brothers), Sonia, Gina and me. We all got along pretty well, except for Gina. That girl just didn't like me and I don't know why? Jackie and Henry were cool but Jackie he stuttered and when he got in trouble and started lying it was awful. He'd tell Mama Green; "S' s'see wa wa we didn't knock the l'l'l'lamp over, it j'j'j'just fell!" Mama Green told me that when I was about a year and half I took my bottle and threw it in the ditch because I decided that it was time to drink out of a cup and I've been drinking out of cups every since. I'll never forget the time when Daddy Green caught me and his grandson Larry doctor when we were five years old. Daddy told mama, Mama Green that is. Boy did they ever put a switch to my behind but they never did tell Mama Florence about that one! That wouldn't have gone over too well with Ma-dear. Then one day a real fancy lady named Marylou sent for me to come live with her and her husband in Washington, D.C. She was one of my mama's older sisters.

With city life came all the things that were apart of Aunt Mary and Uncle Bill's household. Up north Mary had dropped the "Lou." She said it sounded better. My tenure under Aunt Mary's wing lasted up through my adult life. I never called her mama because she didn't want my mama to feel like she was taking her place. But Aunt Mary definitely took on the role! The first thing she did was throw away the wig I wore on the flight from Tennessee. My hair hadn't been properly cared for so it was very short and brittle so Mama Green bought me a wig. I thought it was cute but Aunt Mary didn't seem to think a wig was appropriate for a perfectly healthy seven year old. Her next mission was to grow my hair. She said; "Child, your grandma was part Cherokee Indian. You're supposed to have some hair! She was right! Within months all my hair was long and I had a new attitude. I was even enrolled in the Art Linkletter School of Dance to begin pursuing my dream as a dancer. I had my own room with lots of pretty clothes and we had a pool table in the basement.

My auntie taught me to think twice and speak once. She taught me to be a leader and not a follower. She taught me to strive for the best. Aim for the moon and if you miss you will land among the stars, that's what she said. And she always told me not to be afraid to stand alone. Maybe I should call her Aunt Mama!

As a junior high school student I met yet another mama, Mrs. Cornelia Brown! I used to think she was so mean, but now I know that was because she didn't let those children run over her. Our school was so full of activities; archery, chess, foreign studies, the yearbook staff, the Future Business Leaders of America and a whole lot of other things. Then there was the music department and that's where I met Miss Brown. She first exposed me to the music of Duke Ellington and Leonard Bernstein. She even taught me some songs by Dionne Warwick and The Spinners! She would also frequently come and pick me up in her big gold Cadillac and take me with her to the Kennedy Center. She loved my singing voice but she didn't cut me any slack. She watched everything I did and she even called my house if she didn't like my choice of friends. She said I was different from all those other kids who didn't wanna grow up to *be* something. She used to make me so sick. She was always in my business. Years later I figured out that was all because she loved me.

From that time to now, so many beautiful women have touched my life in so many ways. When I was competing in a beauty contest as a teenager. I met a big beautiful blues singing woman named Rubye. For some reason she was instantly drawn to me. She said I looked like I could be her daughter.
She also said that I just looked like I was going to win the pageant and she was right. After that if she was ever performing at a blues club and I happened to be there, she would call me up on stage to sing the blues with her. It didn't matter that I was only sixteen, I was giggin' with Mama Rubye and she knew how to sing the blues!

With California and college came two whole new issues; Boys and Showbiz! Both meant a whole lot of rejection and growing pains. To soothe those emotional needs and to give advice on all my biological needs was Mama Renee. She lived in the biggest house on her street in Baldwin Hills. Unbeknownst to her, when I first came over to baby-sit her kids I decided that they would never get rid of me. Her husband knew everything in the world about computers and she knew everything about everything! Her middle name had to be Confucius! Renee always listened without judgment. She always provided such loving advice. I'm still convinced that she's a genius.

I met another Mama after I got into the work force and her name is Dr. Mayme Clayton. This soft spoken woman is like a gentie giant of library sciences. As the founder of the Western States Black Research center she has dedicated her life to preserving our history. She has artifacts such as original slave trading papers, rare books and vintage films all right in her back yard. She is so sweet and kind and she always calls me her daughter!

What can I say about my mama Nikki. I don't ever recall anyone calling her mama Nikki before I did but now everybody and their mama is calling mama Nikki, Mama Nikki. I met Nikki through her daughter and they both are such positive and supportive people. I don't exactly remember just when I claimed Nikki as my mama Nikki but I think it was after so many people kept asking if her daughter and I were sisters. Finally we just started telling everybody yes we were. So if Kim was my sister then that had to make Nikki my mama too. Once again God sent me what I needed when I needed it. Mamma Nikki's motivation, encouragement and belief in me and my vision helped launch some of my greatest performances to date. And she is so passionate about her people. This little woman has been the force behind so many projects and no matter what she always keeps going strong! In a world where Christians and Muslims aren't supposed to get along. She showed me unconditional love.

Lastly there is Mama Claudia. There comes a time when the strongest of the strong get tired and feel like they can't go on anymore. I had gotten to such a point and I needed more than a hug, more than a sermon and more than a self help book. I needed answers. That's when I came to know Claudia. She challenged me to go within and release the power of forgiveness. By her loving instruction I found out that I had the power to either permit or dismiss all the negatives in my life. You see I was a church girl and I was shocked that even church girls could feel so low. Miss Claudia gave me a challenge that I'll never forget...go to church every Sunday or go to God everyday?

I'm here because of all my mamas! Oh I didn't forget my Jewish Mama, I love you too Flo! And I love you too Mama Sweeney, you're my church mama! From the first to the last, I love them all and no one could take their place. They brought me through the rough spots and dark places. I am the seed of all of these women. When I shine, it's their reflection that you see. This is my village. These are my mamas. These are all my mamas!

WHEN I DIE I WANT TO BE OOOOOOLD!

When I die I want to be oooold! I mean really, really oooold!!
You see, I don't want any sadness at my funeral. When people hear that I've died, the first thing
I want them to say is; "Well it's about damn time! 'Ain't she 'bout a hundred?" Then I want
another person to cut in saying; "Naw, she gotta be older than that cause she got a grandchild
'bout sixty five!!" And while they're swapping stories another person steps up and overhears
that I've passed away. The third person then chimes in saying; "Shucks, I thought she was dead
already!"

I want to check out of here knowing that my time was well spent and I want everybody
to know it. If I happen to be a widow then I want the chapel buzzin' with rumors about a handsome
forty year old who was said to be keeping me company til my dying day. In fact I want the whole
church chuckling in remembrance of some silly thing that I did at one time or another. AND I DON'T
WANT NOBODY DAMN BODY SINGING PRECIOUS LORD! That song would make an ax
murderer cry. Actually that song by Luther Vandross that says "a chair is still a chair" would be
rather nice.

Of course I want my family there. I want my children and grand children and great, great
grandchildren there and some great, great, great grandchildren too. Midway through the service
I want one of my great-great great grands to whisper to one of their parents and say; "Who was that
lady again Mama?" I don't want no sadness, no broken hearts, no puffy eyes and no dry sermons.
When its time to view the remains (that's the time that everybody usually chokes up), I want to make
my final appearance in a red lace dress with a ruffled collar and a red straw hat with a single red rose
in my stiff brown hands and yes my nails will be red too!

And I don't want to be buried in no diamonds and gold either. That's stupid. Ain't no use in laying up bounty for the grave diggers. If they put anything in my casket with me let it be a picture of Mr. October and a Spiegal Catalogue, in honor of my two favorite past times shopping and drooling at gorgeous men. When I die I want to oooold cause I don't want other folks to feel what I have felt when loved ones have left too soon.

I want the day of my home going to be filled with love and laughter. And to top off my gala departure I want the inscription on my tombstone to read:

> Here lies an old diva,
>
> Who is sometimes known to flirt.
>
> We don't know just how old she is
>
> But some say she's old as dirt.
>
> Never false or phony,
>
> But a loyal, loving friend
>
> Here lies an old diva
>
> grand and gracious til the end.

***Dedicated to my friend Lexi Bigham, who left here way too soon! I love you and I miss you!

THAT'S OKAY HE'S MY BABY

When I met him I felt like the luckiest girl in the world! He was so fine! And he wanted me! I happened to live in a town where the pickings were slim. Now I wasn't hardly desperate or anything like that but I also wasn't about to pass up any opportunities. When we started out dating, we were inseparable. I mean, he couldn't make a move without me. He couldn't. You see his car had kinda conked out a few months before we started dating. But that was okay because I didn't mind helping a brother out from time to time. Even though I thought of myself as that "Essence" kind of a woman. I knew that my black man had a rough time out there dealing with The Man everyday so I supported my man anyway that I could.

My new beau was a hard working man. Everyday when I was hard at work he was busy at home writing poems and circling ads in the Dramalogue magazine and all the while he was developing his plan to get ahead. After we had been spending so much time together it just made sense for him to move in with me. So he did. It was just me and my baby and my gold fish. One day when I came home from work I noticed that he had taken it upon himself to move the furniture around and make the place feel more like home. Then he started answering my phone and getting huffy with my ex-boyfriends like he was actually paying the phone bill or something. But he wasn't afraid of hard work though. Why once he even took a job as one of the street characters at a local theme park. I know this because one of my friends told me that they saw him. But he was my baby and I was his girl. The "ship" that he was waiting on was taking a little long to come in so from time to time I didn't mind chipping in. This man loved me more than anyone ever had and he wanted to marry me.

I didn't think much of it the first time I came home a little late and he seemed a bit antsy. He had a wild look in his eyes when he got this way and he reacted as if I had personally insulted him because my day ran a little long. But that's okay he was my baby, I was his girl and I was going to MAKE this relationship work. I was not going to end up like my other man-less girlfriends.

After a while I grew tired of trying to be this man's all and all. As a black woman I was already used to having the weight of the world on my shoulders and I believed the myth that I could do it all. Even though deep within my gut I could sense that something just didn't feel right. But I knew that as long as I flashed a big, bright and bubbly grin then I could convince even my closest friends that I had found true bliss.

I had kissed a lot of frogs looking for *him*. Whoever *he* was. I had spent so many cozy nights wrapped up in the hope that someone would sweep me away and save me from this lonely confusing abyss that sometimes was my life. Well, I thought I had found him. He was willing to share my life, so this HAD to be him! He had taken the place of my family and friends. And ONLY he mattered! It was like I was hypnotized into his world.

We had come up with a budget for our future plans and he was very adamant about sticking to it. Once I was between pay checks and I asked him for a few dollars for lunch money. He gave me three. Three dollars that is. He also told me that we shouldn't be wasting money on popcorn when we went to the movies. Then I came home one day and my gold fish were dead. He said he didn't know what happened but he also stressed, with that wild look in his eyes, that he had always hated goldfish. I thought; "How can anyone hate goldfish." He seemed to go from the sweetest guy in the world to a raging tyrant within a moments time. But that's okay, he was my baby and I was his girl.

I had never seen a bruise on my body before and part of me didn't even believe that it was there. How could someone who makes me feel so good have done this to me? I was actually afraid of him. It's funny. I had long since learned how to act tuff and fight my way through the work force or defend myself when I was offended or disrespected but this was different. This was a very confusing and embarrassing private battle. What power did this man have over me? He was so menacingly evil in his terrible fits of anger and yet so gentle and so pitiful when he sobbed in remorse. I had alienated my family and friends so who would I go to now? I had been so flip and so confident that my relationship was so different from everyone else's. I just knew that my man would put all the other sad commitment phobic men to shame. But these bruises didn't lie.

Deep inside I knew that it didn't all happen so suddenly. When I met him deep down inside I wondered how could someone this wonderful still be single? Why did all the other girls pass this one by? Within months I knew that this man may not be a very responsible mate but I felt that I could take up the slack. And the more I tried to save him from himself, the more he resented me. He said it made him feel like more of a failure. But he was my baby and I was his girl.

Somewhere my self esteem had slipped. Oh I looked great and I talked a good game but there was a part of me that needed to be put in check. I don't know when I rationalized that it was okay to just accept whatever came along, especially if the package looked good. Maybe I thought that nobody else would ever come along to love me like he did. He wanted me to believe that I couldn't make it without him. But I was already making it. Hell, I was making a way for me and for him too, what was he talking about? Everybody eventually knew that something was wrong with him but I had finally come to grips with the fact that something was wrong with me too. I guess somehow I didn't think that God was mighty enough to take me out of a bad situation and bring about something better. I took more shit off of him than I would have ever taken from my girlfriends and their friendship had already been proven through the years. I had only known this man for a year and he was the ruler of my world. And my world was in a mess.

Now I know that love isn't about struggle. Oh yeah sometimes you may sacrifice and sometimes you may disagree, but if your whole identity is lost then there's a problem. If you're afraid in your own home then there is a problem and the problem is not just with the one who is inflicting the pain. There's a problem in you too. If you're covering up bruises with make up or making excuses for someone else's irresponsibility then you don't really know what love is at all. Two desperate people clinging together is not love. True love is about balance. It's about having the courage to say yes to what you want and saying no to what you don't want. True love is knowing that before you can save anyone else you must
first save yourself. But first you must love yourself. You must love yourself enough to be the last single woman on earth before you would stay in a relationship where someone abuses you. You must love yourself enough to live in a shelter before you would dwell in a mansion where you are afraid to sleep at night. You must love yourself enough to reject the false impressions of guilt that have been directed to you. You can't save anyone. You can only offer love and support, but that does not include being on the receiving end of their abusive behavior. No one can abuse you unless are there.

That stormy romance finally came to a close. I had to relocate and start a new. All the bruises have healed now and I've met some wonderful suitors. I still think back on all that I went through in that relationship. It taught me a lot. But I can't be mad at him for it, cause hey, I was his girl and *he* was my baby!

RAPE IS THE ISSUE

(Bailiff, Victim and three robed judges, all female. The judges almost overlap their dialogue)

Bailiff: We will now hear rape case #3693.   The honorable Judge Celestine Guy presiding.
          All rise!

Victim: Uhm, your honor it took a while for me to come forth and press charges against my
          attacker because...uhm, well I heard that sometimes the court system is rather hard on
          women and uhm......well,...I didn't think anyone would believe me...you see...

Judge 1: Did you know him?

Judge 2: Had you seen him before?

Judge 3: Were you wearing cologne?

Judge 2: Had you seen him before?

Victim: This is rather hard for me. They said no one would believe me. Yes. I knew who he
          was but he had no right to do what he did to me?

Judge 1: Were you wearing a skirt?

Judge 2: Were your clothes too tight?

Judge 3: Did you have panties on?

Judge 2:   Were your clothes too tight?

Victim: What are you talking about were my clothes too tight? You're a woman you're
          supposed to understand? Nuns get raped, children get raped, innocent unsuspecting
          school teachers get raped!! Where is your head? What are you saying...that only those
          who are raped under certain circumstances are true victims?

Judge 3: What time did he come over?

Judge 1: Do you have a job?

Judge 2: Does this man have *money?*

Judge 1: Do you have a job?

Judge 1,2 &3: Do you want his money?

Victim: The man took me by force! He held me down and no matter how I fought and kicked
          and scratched he just kept on ripping my clothes off. The more I screamed the more
          excited he became. I was in pain!!! It was hurting me!!! And No!! I didn't want his
          goddamn money!

Judge 1:   Are you a loose woman?

Judge 2:   Did you let him kiss you?

Judge 3:   Do you know this man is a hero?

Victim: My body still trembles in terror when I think of what he did to me? Just because he was bigger and stronger gave him no right to have his way with me! I told him no! And I screamed....I screamed so loud that it hurt....nooo! NOOO!!! You can't do this to me!

Judge 1:   It's all very simple...

Judge 2:   You must be a slut.

Judge 3:   It's all very simple.

Victim: I want to thank you for your understanding. I want to thank you for making it clear that I am somehow responsible for every sexually illicit pervert that has ever walked the face of the earth. It's because of You that these perverts go free! But I want to say something else while I've got the floor and maybe you can tell this to some of your sons and grandsons along the way; I don't care what the hour of the day or night may be. And I don't care if a woman has on a judicial robe or if she's just gotten out of the bath tub, NO means NO! If I decide to give it up then that's my choice. If I decide to change my mind, then that's also my choice but No man has the right to take this from me. Not now, not ever!

Judge 1:   It's all very simple. No Means NO.

Judge 2:   It's all very simple. No Means NO.

Judge 3:   It's all very simple. No Means NO.

Judge 1,2 &3: It's all very ...

Victim: Simple. No means no.

THE DAY OF THE MILLION MAN MARCH

I had heard about it but I didn't know what to expect. I knew of a few guys that were going but I wasn't extremely close to anyone who was directly involved. I couldn't escape all the controversy surrounding it and I personally I kept my views to myself. I just hoped that whatever happened was positive. My boyfriend was already a responsible hard working black man and I was very proud of him. He was not able to make it to Washington but we talked about it and he had my support for whatever he decided to do. As a woman I didn't feel left out or slighted in any way because the invitation was only extended to men. Woman have had many forums and platforms in which they could collectively solve their issues. I thought it was a very powerful sentiment for men to get together and confront their own issues of healing and empowerment. Besides in my opinion if the black woman alone was capable of healing the black man, he would have been healed long ago as much as she loves him. And God knows the black woman loves her black man. Even though I didn't know the full scope of the event. I knew that this was something that black man could only get from other black men.

I had recently began working as a contract player in a new television series and I had to be on the set that day so I took my portable TV and put it in my dressing room. There were only two black men who worked on the production crew. I let them know that I had a TV in my room if they wanted to watch it when they got a break. The filming day began early and it was a few hours before I got a chance to turn on the tube! As soon as the screen came in focus, chills broke out all over my body and tears filled my eyes! I flipped from station to station and on every channel it was the same. It was a sea of beautiful black men. These were all the great great grandsons of slaves! I had never seen so many black men together in my life! I kept thinking; "there they are!!" There are all the husbands we've been praying for, there they are! There are all of our brothers and cousins and neighbors! And I also wondered if the father that I haven't seen since I was five years old was out there too.

I spoke softly to the screen; "Are you out there daddy? I'm here and I'm doing okay. If you are out there daddy, please come look for me, I want to see you. Are you out there daddy?" My time was limited. In minutes I would have to perk up and be back before the cameras. I rushed to get in a few phone calls. Mama Nikki's phone was ringing off the hook. She had a call on the other line. I had to connect with some of my sisters to see if they felt the same thing I was feeling. I got Myra on the phone and told her; "Girl, look at all of them men! Next year we're goin' in drag so we can collect some phone numbers!" Myra said she was gonna go and collect child support.

There was a knock on my door followed by the standard five minute warning. Oh my God, please don't let any non-black person say anything to me about this march. I just don't feel like explaining the past two hundred years in five minutes. God was truly on my side, I was treated with the usual respect and courtesy. I don't know what everyone else felt but no one took issue with me. Then one of the older players on the show brought up the subject when we were back in the make up room. Which led to the hair stylist asking me how I felt. I sensed the sincerity of their questions so I took a deep breath and searched my heart for an answer. At first I wanted to shut them out and not even make any conversation. But then I reconsidered. I would rather that they hear my side than simply what a news reporter has to say. And they listened with compassion. Then my senior cast member shared a story of his own about how he had attended the March on Washington with his mother when he was a boy. He told me how his father had thrown a man out of his house for having requested that he sign a petition to oust a new black family that had moved to the neighborhood. He said that his father had threatened him with physical force if he ever heard that his son played any role in bigotry and hate. He told me that he remembered the I Have A Dream speech because he was there!

As I went back to work and looked across a mass of pale faces, I asked myself; "How can I tell who is my friend and who is my enemy just by looking at them?" I have to talk to a man and see his actions before I can truly determine the condition of his heart. I made it a point to contact a few of the most cherished black men that I know. I made it a point to tell them that I thought that they were *one* in a million not just for that day but for always!

MY THIGH MOVED

One day it moved. There I was standing in the dressing room mirror wondering how my legs got so ashy since I last put some lotion on and then...it moved. I know it moved because I saw it. MY THIGH MOVED! I knew I wasn't a teenager anymore.....and I know that the last gym I went to was Mr. Jim's bar-b-que over on the East Side. But there I was an unsuspecting customer eagerly about to try on a size two skirt and then I saw it move. I wouldn't actually say that it jiggled but it sort of moved back and forth...and back and forth...and yeah, I guess you could say it ...jiggled *but just a little bit*. I thought; "When did this happen?" I was supposed to be young and fine *forever!* I stared and stared in the looking glass-- times three! There were three different views of ashy thighs, soft to the touch with just a hint of motion, mind you. Then I made the mistake of turning around. That's when I say THEM! There were dimples back there and no one was smiling!! "AWWWW!"

I screamed. The little anorexic salesgirl tapped on the door; 'Is everything all right? Do you want me to bring a bigger size? We have the same skirt in a size four.' "Everything is just fine, sweety. Thank You." I didn't want a size four, I wanted the size TWO! On second thought, I didn't want to try on those clothes any old way. I was still trying to figure out when my thigh decided that it was going to move. I threw on my clothes, marched out of that dressing room and made my way to my car. And that's when another shocking discovery occurred to me. My thigh wasn't the only thing moving! I could feel my butt trying to get in on the action. Every time *I* moved *it* moved. Lord have mercy what is happening to me? When did my booty start to move? Now I'm gonna have to buy some of those big bloomers with the elastic in them!! Damn! It actually felt like something was in my back pocket. And it *was* something in my back pocket! It was *me*! All me!! Just moving and jiggling like a bowl of Jell-O pudding and Bill Cosby was nowhere to be found! If I wasn't careful I would end up like those ladies who work at the bank. You know those ladies that work at the bank. The ones who are about four foot ten and they're usually the ones who come from the back to approve your transaction. You can tell when they're coming cause you can hear the girdle scoots before they get there. It makes you kinda wonder how anybody could get all of that flesh in a polyester skirt?

But who am I to sneer? Who am I to poke fun or point at anyone else? I am now a member of the calorie counters, the fat burners, the consumers of all the Lean Cuisines and those who STARE at the stair master and wonder; "Why did I buy that thing? I never use it!" I am now a collector of videos that I watch two or three times before tossing them into a pile of dusty aerobic cartridges.

Yes, this brick house may be slowly turning into brick condominiums but when the going gets tough and the tough can't go shopping anymore because there isn't a Lane Bryant in her neighborhood; then I will boldly face the scales, embrace elastic waist lines, stand bravely in a three way mirror and proclaim that I am truly one of the movers and shakers of the world!

ANGRY BLACK WOMAN'S POEM/TALK SHOW SATIRE
(This piece is meant to be exaggerated. This is a satire of all the existing "my man done me
  wrong poems." African or Plantation attire is suggested. The pieces may be performed in
  succession or separately.)

Actress #1:   I, I said I, I gave to you all that I had to give to you...because you, you needed me to.

You said that I was the sun and I was the moon. And together we were the moon and the sun, we had

so much fun.   And we were on the run from Mr. Charlie and his oppressive system!   Just you and me,

and the moon and the sun....on the run.

    You were my Ebony Prince and I was your Nubian Goddess.   I nursed you with the fruits

of my nimble body and when you needed a way to get to work, I gave you a ride in my car, but

we didn't get far, cause I ran out of gas.   And there we were walking to the gas station and then

you Left me! Yes you did you LEFT ME!   You left me for a woman who wears BRAIDS!!

Beads, bangles and BRAIDS!!   You black son of Baptist. How dare you leave your Egyptian

high priestess, the mother of the universe, the mother of three of your ten kids. I HATE YOU!!

I HATE YOU! I HATE YOUR BAD ASS KIDS AND I HATE YOUR MAMA TOO!   AND

I HATE MR. CHARLIE!!   Torn out of mother Africa like a suckling babe I was brought here to

build this nation for free, and I want my mule, WHERE IS MY MULE?   The sun, the moon,

the earth, the trees, Mr. Charlie, your bad ass kids and My Mule!!   I have been ROBBED!!!

And now I'm gon' kill you, cause I'm mad!!!

(another well dressed actress steps on stage)

ACTRESS #2: Hey sister, you need to let it go.

ANGRY BLACK WOMAN: And who are you?

que: talk show theme music
ACTRESS #2: I'm Ricky, Jenny, Jerry, Raphael Lake and today we're talking
                    with angry black women.

(segue into part two of the scene) Actress #1 is now seated and becomes the guest and actress #2
becomes the hostess. they are joined by four or more other actresses.

TALK SHOW AUDIENCES/THAT IS NOT US!

HOSTESS: Hello everyone and welcome to the show. For those of you who don't know I'm Ricky, Jenny, Jerry, Raphael, Lake. And today we're talking with angry black women. So what is this about you hating Mr. Charlie, I mean why would anyone want to hate him?

GUEST: (very ghetto) Okay well first of all, this here ain't all about Mr. Charlie, see. See, my man was goin' all off on me and stuff on account of my car running out of gas.

AUDIENCE MEMBER #1: Esscuuusse me, but what I wanna know is why come yo man don't have no "coar." When I was with him, he had a "coar!" Okay! So you mus' not be on yo job as a black woman!

AUDIENCE MEMBER #2: Okay first of all, we is on TV and we don't need to be makin' ratings for these folks by showing them how ignorant we is! I happen to have a very good relationship with my man.

AUDIENCE MEMBER #3: Oh no she didn't! I know she didn't try to go there?! Ricky, Jenny, Jerry, Raphael, Lake why don't you *axe* her where her man at?

HOSTESS: Well tell us Shaniqua Shante, where is yo man at?

AUDIENCE MEMBER #2: He in jail. But he gettin' out soon.
(Audience reacts)

AUDIENCE MEMBER #1: All y'all heifers need to get yo act together cause y'all can't tell me shit 'bout my life!

AUDIENCE MEMBER #3: Who you callin' a heifer? With all them kids you got by all them different daddies you need to shut up!

(The audience begins hurling insults at each other in an outrageous fashion. The guest then gets up and walks down stage, past the arguing crowd and turns off an imaginary TV set. When she turns off the TV set the other players freeze in place. She then removes the wrap from her hair and if she's wearing big gaudy earrings, she removes them too. Her manner is very calm and sophisticated.)

GUEST: This is not who we are, at least this is not totally representative of who we are.
(One by one the other players come back to life but in a calm and articulate manner)

AUDIENCE MEMBER #1: Now I know what you've seen...

AUDIENCE MEMBER #2: And I know what you've heard...

HOST: And I know that you've been entertained.......

AUDIENCE MEMBER #3: And I know that many of you would like to think that that is the way we all are.

GUEST: But that's not who we are.

THE LATITUDES OF ATTITUDES
(Can be done by one or more actresses)

What she said was; "Get outta here! I wouldn't take your stupid ass back if you begged me!"

But what she meant was; "You have hurt me and I'm afraid to trust you again."

What she said was; "You broke and you ain't got shit, so what I need you for?"

But what she meant was; "I am struggling just like you and I need somebody to
help me in this struggle!"

What she said was; "Your sorry behind should never left in the first place!"

But what she meant was; "Why is it that the men always get to leave? I'm tired
and I wanna leave too but there is nowhere for me to go."

What she said was; "That's your child, not mine so however y'all make it, is up to you! It ain't
got a damn thing to do with me!!"

But what she meant was; "You have laid with another woman all while I was loving you
and now you expect me to take care of a child of which I have
no part; a child filled with half of the blood of a man that I once
loved and the other half of a woman who hates me.!"

What she said was; "You know what? I don't need you! I don't need anybody like you!
You're nothing!"

But what she meant was; "Since you forced me to get along without you, now I've discovered
that 'gettin along without you ain't so bad afterall!"

What she said was; " I hope you crawl your stinky low life no good carcass into a hole and die!"

But what she meant was; "You have hurt me so deeply and I want you to feel the same
pain that you have made me feel. And the only thing I can use
to hurt you right now....is words.

The Latitudes of Attitudes.

WHITE GIRLS/BLACK GUYS

It used to hurt me so bad when I would see a black guy with a white girl. Of course I grew up in the shadow of the dream where one day we would all live in a nation where we would not be judged by the color of our skin but by the content of our character, but somehow every time I saw one of my fine, successful brothers all hugged up with a blonde, blue eyed super model, I somehow felt that he had personally rejected me. Now if I saw a white girl with a dumpy, funny looking fellow then that didn't seem to bother me so bad. I figured, shoot; "I didn't want him anyway." These are the facts and this is the ugly truth. I felt like every black man who chose a white woman over me; was rejecting not only me, but he was rejecting a part of his own flesh. I felt like he was rejecting his mama and his grandmama and his sisters and every black woman on earth. I didn't know how badly damaged I was by the subliminal. The subtle pretext that in this country I was not good enough. The subconscious programming that the pure blooded offspring of the plantation Negro was simply unacceptable for today's "successful" man. To offset this myriad of emotions was the locker room mentality that the black woman had somehow become too difficult, too taxing for a brother to handle! There was this notion that she was too "demanding." Is this new? Did some brother think this up all by himself? Every black woman that I know has always been demanding! She has demanded that I be the very best that I can be. She has demanded that I never half step my responsibilities for she knew that I would grow up in a world that sees color first. And she knew that to be black meant that you had to be twice as good just to be considered equal. Still I was plagued by this gentle piercing every time I saw a happy loving couple of ebony and ivory strolling beside me. I felt like; 'everyone else in the world is rejecting me, why are you rejecting me too brother?' Since we're speaking frankly, I must tell you the truth. Even though I walked tall and proud and I might even have flashed a warm smile this is the sad sentiment that I carried home to my empty apartment. My mouth couldn't form the words but I could hear the utterance in my heart; 'they have taken everything else from us and now she wants him too.' Does she understand you like I do? Will she stick by you like I will? Will she be there when your money is gone? Does she know your pain?

This is definitely not the kind of confession I would make standing up in church. I am fighting against prejudice and racism but why did this hurt so bad? Why didn't I just go out and get me a fine, successful white man? You know most sisters have a closet fantasy about somebody. They won't admit it but most every sister has said at one time or another; "Girl, he's so fine, I'd cross the color line for him!" For me, it'd have to be Dallas Reins, the weather man or Pat Reiley. But even if I did, every time I saw those TV documentaries or every time there would be a re-run of Roots it would be difficult when it was time to get in the same bed and cuddle with him without wondering if this was my slave master's great great grandson? Did this man want me for me or was he trying to live out some fantasy? It was just too much to contemplate.

I'm not in that place anymore. I celebrate with those who have found a true and lasting love no matter what their unique circumstances happen to be. I am proud of the skin I'm in and not even two centuries of degrading conditions can convince me that I am anything short of a beautiful and divine creation of God. Whatever man did not choose me was not mine and was never meant to be mine. Life is about choices. And I choose those who choose me. So go ahead my brother. Go live in peace and happiness. No harm, no foul. (beat) Just don't let me catch you looking out the corner of your eye.

A DIFFERENT KIND OF BLACK MAN

THOUGH YOU ARE SHOWN ON TV SCREENS
HAND CUFFED, CHAINED & DISGRACED,
THOUGH YOUR FAILURES ARE EXPLOITED
AND CONSTANTLY THROWN IN YOUR FACE,
I'VE KNOWN A DIFFERENT KIND OF BLACK MAN.

THOUGH YOUR ENEMIES WOULD LIKE YOU TO THINK
THAT YOU ARE ALL WORTHLESS AND NO GOOD;
PLASTIC CAPPED, GOLD CHAIN WEARING HOODLUMS
HANGING 'ROUND THE HOOD.
I'VE KNOWN A DIFFERENT KIND OF BLACK MAN.

THOUGH THE MOVIES THAT YOUNG BLACK BOYS SEE,
SHOW MOSTLY DIPPING AND SWAYING AND
"NO OFFICER, IT WASN'T ME."
I'VE KNOWN A DIFFERENT KIND OF BLACK MAN.

THOUGH THE DAILY NEWS SHOWS AN OVERLOAD
OF BROTHERS PULLING TRIGGERS ON THEIR OWN,
I'VE KNOWN A DIFFERENT KIND OF BLACK MAN.

AND THOUGH SOME SISTERS SHARE A COMMON BOND
CAUSE SOME OLD DOG DID SOMEBODY WRONG,
I'VE KNOWN A DIFFERENT KIND OF BLACK MAN.

THOUGH SOME HAVE LEFT THEIR FAMILIES
NEVER TO RETURN
AND SOME HAVE CAST THEIR FUTURE
DOWN THE GLASS PIPE TO BURN,
I'VE KNOWN A DIFFERENT KIND OF BLACK MAN.

A DIFFERENT KIND OF BLACK MAN HAS TOUCHED MY SOUL
AND EMBRACED ME WITH LOVE AND CONCERN.
HAILES, JOHNSONS, BROOKS AND DORSEYS
HAVE ALL HELPED ME TO LEARN.

A DIFFERENT KIND OF BLACK MAN
REACHED OUT AND GRABBED MY HAND;
WHEN I WAS YEARNING FOR DIRECTION
GREENS, SMITHS AND TAYLORS
HELPED ME TO UNDERSTAND.

HENDERSONS, WASHINGTONS,
HINES AND LEAKES
HELPED MY DELICATE HEART
REACH ITS PEAK;

BROWNS, MIALS AND UNDERWOODS
HAVE ALL REASSURED ME
THAT THE BLACK MAN STILL HAS MUCH GOOD.

I'VE KNOWN THE MAN WHO PUTS GOD FIRST
AND TRAVELS WITH A MISSION;
I'VE KNOWN THE MAN WHO PRAYS EACH NIGHT
TO HELP THE EARTH'S CONDITION.

I'VE KNOWN THE MAN WHO IS CAREFUL
FOR HE CARRIES THE SEED
OF UNBORN GENERATIONS
WAITING TO BE BORN IN ME.

I'VE KNOWN THE MAN CALLED FRIENDS AND LOVERS,
FATHERS, UNCLES,
SONS AND BROTHERS;
CHALLENGING THE SYSTEM, REWORKING THE PLAN,
I'VE KNOWN A DIFFERENT KIND OF BLACK MAN.

NEVER MIND

Today I must write a letter to God. It's a grievance letter, a letter of complaint if you will. You see I want to let You know just how outraged I am at the way that things are going in my life. After all I have a master plan of where I think my life should be by now and well, this present state just isn't cutting it. There are just too many things that clutter my mind fields and send my frustration levels skyrocketing. Frankly God, I think that You can do better! Excuse me, while I get the phone. Oh it's a call from a friend to say hello and that they were thinking of me and wanting to see how I was doing. Well I'm doing fine, I guess.... anyway I'm busy now I've got to finish this letter to God.

Okay God where were we? Oh yes, I feel that you need some help up there because surely you don't recognize the magnitude of my problems. For starters I... oh damn, that's the phone again. I'll be right back.

Hello? You have a delivery for me? All right I'll buzz you in. Now what can this be? Oh, that's the door. Hi. Yes, it is a nice day isn't it? Where do you want me to sign? Wow, look at the size of this box! I gotta open this right now. Ahhh how sweet. It's another little present for my baby from a friend far away.

Whew, that was so thoughtful but I've got to get back to my letter. Dearest God. Oh that's so formal. Dear Great Master of the universe. No, that's even worse. How about Hey God, what's up? I know you said I might go through some things but this is RIDICULOUS and FURTHERMORE... I can't believe this it's the phone again.

Yes? I mean hello who's speaking? Nooo. No way? Where in the world have you been? How did you get my number. I had been trying to reach you. Boy did we a lot of fun back in the day. Remember when we all went to.... (listening) Yes, of course I remember. I never laughed so hard in all of my life. And how is Charles? What? When did he die? How about Neicy and Ricky? Them too? BOTH of them? You're kidding? What happened to their children? Their children went to THAT school? Were they there the day of the shooting? Oh no!! Are they okay now? That's a relief but Mrs. Grayson is too old to take care of them. Whatever happened to Danny? No he didn't. When is he getting out? Whoa that's kind of hard to believe. Are you coming to the reunion? Hey, whatever the case, you keep in touch okay. I know we always say that we will but let's do it this time. All right now. Bye.

Neicy and Ricky? Gone? And Charles too? I can't believe crazy old Charlie Mac isn't still walking around here. And those cute little children. What a life. Whew. Let's see now where was I? Oh yeah. Dear God, Why haven't you answered all of my prayers yet. I have been asking you for certain things for a very long time and I have been patient. I just don't know why you let me suffer like this.

Oh no, not again. Hello? Oh hi, Dr. Porter. Oh I'm fine, what's the reason for your call? All my test results are negative? Good, yeah I know about drinking more water and eating more fresh fruits and vegetables. Is that it? Well you take care too. I'll see you in six months.

Dear God, NEVER MIND.

TRUST

Do you know of the times when you have prayed for something so long and waited for something so long that it seemed like it would take a miracle of God to manifest something special in your life. And then the thing happens. The blessing the gift, the miracle that you've waited for so long to finally comes to pass. You celebrate, you jump for joy, you share your bliss with your friends and family. And then you realize that this very blessing comes with great responsibilities, perhaps even greater than you've ever known. It comes with challenges far more vast than you've ever seen before and then you catch yourself in between the bliss, wondering what's next. What will I do? What can I do? Am I ready for this? Then you return to the very God that you had prayed to in the beginning for the blessing, except now you're begging for more answers. You're begging for a sign, a clue, a definite road map outlining what's going to happen next. And there is none. There is only an overwhelming impulse to wallow in a blank state of being because answers, definite answers are too hard to contemplate. The future is now the present and tomorrow is fast approaching. Then there's another faint beckoning which pulls on your psyche making a steady but limp attempt to break your dissolution and return you to a place of trust. Not trust in anything that you physically see or know but trust in the highest being, the greatest consciousness, the almighty force of the universe,
the God force. You see, there are times when your only solid option is to trust. The times when there's no turning back and the choices have been made and there's no clear picture, these are the times to trust. There is no other sane option than to trust. You must trust with the same kind of trust that allows you to lie down on Monday, expecting that the next day there will be a Tuesday. Its the kind of trust that lets you walk down the street with confidence that the sun will hold its place firmly in the sky and illuminate your day and that it will not fall down and ignite you. It's trust that flowers will keep blooming and plants will keep growing and animals will keep reproducing to replenish the earth so that man's existence will continue. The answer is trust. Blindly trust. Simply trust. Only trust. Trust

BAGGAGE CLAIM IS TO THE LEFT

Welcome aboard Flight Relationships where you're in for the ride of your life. I'm Miss Leading and I'll be your chief flight attendant until we reach our destination of eternal bliss. Our Captain I. B Romeo and our first mate N.O. Cassanova extend the warmest of greetings to all who have dared to board this aircraft.

We do hope that you are fully insured because we are not responsible for any casualties along the way including hurt feelings, unmet expectations or any monetary damages that you may incur. We do however wish you courageous souls a long and happy excursion. Here on Flight Relationships there are a few rules.

First, you are responsible for finding out the flight history of your mate prior to take off. It is up to you to determine if your mate has previously flown solo or if there are past experiences of crash landings or crash and burns.

Rule number two: There is to be no throwing of mates out of the aircraft once we are airborne. If you find that there is someone that you'd like to throw off the plane right now; well then that is perfectly allowed.

But remember this airline is in no ways liable for any insult or injury. You are completely responsible for who you have chosen.

Rule number three: Please buckle up and adhere to all safety precautions, there could be unexpected turbulence... a lot of turbulence..., a *whole* lot of turbulence. That's to be expected on Flight Relationships but please refrain from using expletives and mean references to family members.

Should there be a drop in cabin pressure, relax.... it's just the realization that the person you're flying with is not who you thought they were... and you're not who they thought you were either. You don't need a mask, or oxygen it's just a nice little reality check point.

Most importantly is Rule number four: Baggage Claim Is To The Left. We understand that Flight Relationships could be a long journey for some and a short haul for others. We also know that you have to take some things with you but UNNECESSARY CARGO IS STRICTLY PROHIBITED. Baggage Claim is to the left! Please, everyone step off of the plane, look to the left and observe this area. We will wait for you. This is a specially designated spot for all of that bullshhhh..... um, all of those "items" that should be left behind!

On Flight Relationships all baggage that cannot be stowed neatly beneath the seat in front of you or in the overhead compartment MUST BE CHECKED. We have no room for this extra stuff. It will only get in our way, impede our progress and slow us down from our new destination. Please, I must tell you one more time, Baggage Claim Is To The Left.

Look around the cabin, check your neighbor's seat. Are there things sticking out, bulging out, held together by safety pins and tape? Well it's not going away once we're airborne. Get rid of it now, free your load, Baggage Claim is to the left!

SOMEONE MURDERED JUNE CLEVER

Fast forward past the prim and innocent, the always smiling, dainty hostess and maternal maiden June Cleaver. I'm sorry to report that she is dead. They killed her and her starched little apron, A line dress and perfect hair. Who was this white broad anyway? She once was me, except the white part that is. The consummate caretaker and nurturer, full time problem solder, cook, serologist and maid. Why I've never seen anyone so damn happy to have a dust rag in her hand. Ah, and the painted smile and up do with scents of White Rain, Adorn or Dippity Do. Well Ms. June Clever has been assassinated. With great lamentation I must announce that she is deceased.

She could not hold up under the demands and expectations placed upon her. Her rebounding skills have failed and she is now only a memory, a rerun on Nick At Night, she's a figment of television past. For if Ms. Clever were to live on then her lines would all be changed and her costume would be less than perfect. We should just put out an all points bulletin for anyone with any information on the murder of June Clever. Evidence suggests that the killer did not act alone. We suspect a conspiracy. There are many who may be responsible for this. Ms. Clever was such a perky soul. Also found in this tragedy were her wire framed rose colored glasses. They appear to have been crushed by the harsh realities of modern life. Another unusual item that was found at at the scene of the crime was a date book, a palm pilot, a cell phone, a pager, a fax machine, a computer with a CD ROM and a lot of self help books... and tapes.

It seems that Ms. Clever had over exerted herself trying to be too many things to too many people. We also looked in the refrigerator and found no fresh vegetables only frozen packages of fat free microwavable food and all of the water was in bottles. This was very unlike June. Her garden had been replaced by a Jacuzzi but there was no water in it. The killer or killers must have known that Mrs. Clever craved relaxation so they deprived her of it. What a tragic end for dear June. We must all cherish her plastic memory and beware of copy cat killers.

Dear, dear June, dear dead June, your life was not in vain. While your murder is still being investigated, I did hear that they are going to remake your famous show. They have only to cast your part. After auditioning thousands, it's a toss up between Rosanne and Rupaul. Dear, dear June, we'll really miss you.

MY BUTT DROPPED

It's there but not like it used to be, you see it's hanging lower, a little softer and a little more subtle than it's former robust posture. You see my butt dropped.

My derriere is now just some meat and muscle in a pair of pants instead of the *taw-dow* that it used to be. My 'pumps in a bump' is now a 'rump and a hump' and this is making me very sad. My onion that used to make men cry, now makes me cry. It's sagging' y'all. My butt dropped. It's still there, it's still an ass mind you but I didn't know a butt could change so much. It feels more like cargo than a caboose. Gravity has pulled this once prized gluteus maximum just a bit further South. South of the Border. My ass sits where my assets used to be.

I'M SORRY MRS. PHELPS

I'm sorry Mrs. Phelps. I didn't understand. I took one look at you and determined that surely you must have missed something. Without the benefit of a proper investigation I whole heartedly concluded that you and your run down appearance was due to a lack of will, a lack of esteem and a mis-guidance of focus. Never did I imagine that the absence of any deliberate grooming and personal style was due to the fact that maybe at the end of the day you had given so much to so many that there was nothing left for you to put back into you. I completely overlooked the possibility that after the family budget, there was no budget to beautify and no energy left to rectify. Mrs. Phelps how ignorant I was to comment on your pace and the fatigue in your face and your thrown together appearance. Mrs. Phelps, I'm sorry.

Again and again I'm sorry because now I realize that even though I'd like to see you do better and look better and feel better, well maybe this is the best you can do. I now see that your simplicity makes you even more beautiful than any superficial cosmetic enhancement. So Mrs. Phelps, I wish you rest because you need it, I wish you wealth because you could use it and I wish warm and thoughtful comfort because you deserve it. Here's a rose and a pair of my shoes. In exchange I'll gladly take a pair of your shoes, I'm certain they're a lot more comfortable than mine. Keep on stepping Mrs. Phelps, again I say I'm sorry.

I'M SORRY ANGRY BLACK WOMAN

I'M SORRY ANGRY BLACK WOMAN, I'M SORRY! GIRL I DIDN'T KNOW WHAT YOU WERE GOING THROUGH! NOW A WHILE BACK I MADE A FEW COMMENTS ABOUT THE ANGRY BLACK WOMAN. YOU KNOW THE SISTER WHO'S ABOUT TWO MINUTES OFF OF ANYBODY'S BEHIND., THE ANGRY SISTER WHO WORKS AT THE CUSTOMER SERVICE COUNTER AND SHE LOOKS LIKE SHE'S MAD AT YOU BECAUSE IT'S YOUR FAULT THAT SHE HAD TO COME TO WORK TODAY. I'M TALKING ABOUT THE WOMAN WHO'S GOT PMS AND BAD CRAMPS EVERYDAY!! CAN I GET AN AMEN FOR THE BUS DRIVER WHO'S PERCHED UPON HER HIGH CHAIR ROARING TO BITE SOMEBODY'S HEAD OFF BECAUSE SHE'S GOT TO WORK A DOUBLE SHIFT WITH A SERIOUS CASE OF HEMORRHOIDS AND SHE JUST BROKE A NAIL WHILE TRYING TO MAKE A U-TURN IN RUSH HOUR. I'M SENDING A SHOUT OUT TO THE WAITRESS WHOSE FEET HURT AND SHE JUST GOT A RUN IN HER STOCKING... AND HERE YOU ARE TAKING ALL DAMN DAY TO MAKE UP YOUR MIND WHETHER YOU WANT POTATO SALAD OR COLE SLAW WITH YOUR BABY BACK RIBS!!

I AM APOLOGIZING TO ALL THE ANGRY BLACK WOMEN BECAUSE NOW I KNOW THAT SOMETIMES WHEN YOU'VE WORKED ALL DAY, RUSHED HOME TO COOK BUT YOUR KIDS DON'T LIKE THE FOOD, YOUR HUSBAND DIDN'T MOP THE FLOOR, YOUR UNCLE WILLIE DIDN'T PAY YOU BACK, THE DOG ATE JUNIOR'S HOMEWORK AND THE BABY POURED ALL THE BUBBLE BATH IN THE RUG AND REFUSED TO GO TO SLEEP UNTIL AT TEN THIRTY.

NOPE YOU HAVEN'T SAT DOWN YET AND NOW IT'S TIME FOR SOME HUGGING, TIME FOR SOME LOVING, TIME FOR SOME STEAMY OHH LAA LAA AND I KNOW WHAT YOU'RE THINKING, MY MAN MUST BE PSYCHIC, HE READ MY MIND AND NOW ALAS, I SHALL GO TO SLEEP BUT

WHAT'S THAT? OH GOODIE THE BABY'S AWAKE AGAIN? OH NO SWEETIE, YOU JUST LIE THERE IN YOUR STATE OF RIGORMORTIS, I'LL GET UP AND CHECK ON BOOBIE. WHAT'S THAT? WELL IF IT ISN'T THE ALARM CLOCK! HOW ABOUT I GET THE BREAKFAST, GET THE KIDS TO SCHOOL, NOW IT'S OFF TO THE JOB, I'M TIRED ALREADY AND I HAVEN'T EVEN GOTTEN TO WORK YET. AM I HAVING A DEJA VOUS HERE? WELL PARDON ME IF MY SOCIAL SKILLS ARE NOT ALL TOGETHER IN TACT, IF I HAPPEN TO COME UP A FEW VOTES SHY IN THE MISS CONGENIALITY CONTEST AND IF MY MERE EXPRESSION SAYS 'TALK TO THE HAND!' BECAUSE MISS ATTITUDE DOESN'T UNDERSTAND SO YES I APOLOGIZE ANGRY BLACK WOMAN YOU'VE HAD TO WEAR TOO MANY HATS, FIGHT TOO MANY BATTLES, PAY TOO MANY DEBTS, BEAR TOO MANY HURTS AND NOW YOUR ALMIGHTY ATTITUDE IS YOUR ARMOR, YOUR PROTECTIVE GEAR TO LET THE WORLD KNOW HOW TOUGH YOU ARE, TO LET THE WORLD KNOW YOU'RE NOT HAVING IT? NO DISRESPECT AND NO DRAMA UNLESS OF COURSE YOU'RE GIVING IT... DRAMA THAT IS. SO HEY ONCE AGAIN, ANGRY BLACK WOMAN, I'M SORRY FOR JUDGING YOU, SIZING YOU UP AND COMMENTING ON YOUR DISPOSITION BUT DON'T LET IT GO TO YOUR HEAD BECAUSE NEXT TIME I MIGHT HAVE TO GO OFF ON *YOU!*

HELP, MY TODDLER'S TRYING TO KILL ME!

HELP! HE'S TRYING TO KILL ME! I KNOW THAT I AM A VICTIM OF DOMESTIC ABUSE.
YOU SEE MY ATTACKER STARTS EARLY IN THE MORNING, SCREAMING, CRYING, DEMANDING,
THROWING THINGS, SCRATCHING MY FACE AND PULLING MY HAIR. YEP, I'VE GOT THIS THING
TOTALLY FIGURED. HE'S TRYING TO KILL ME.

MY TODDLER THAT IS. I DIDN'T KNOW THAT A TWO YEAR OLD COULD BE SO DEMANDING. IT'S
TERRIBLE ISN'T IT? EACH DAY HE GROWS STRONGER, MORE CHARMING, MORE ABLE TO LURE
ME INTO DOING THINGS HIS WAY. HE YELLS AT ME, HE BLURTS OBSCENITIES, MOSTLY IN
BABY TALK BUT STILL IT HURTS.

PART OF THE PLAN IS TO UNDERMINE MY DEFENSE MECHANISMS THROUGH SLEEP
DEPRIVATION. IT USUALLY STARTS AT ABOUT SIX MONTHS INTO THE PREGNANCY. NO NIGHT
AFTER THAT WILL EVER BE THE SAME. IT WILL BE A LONG TIME BEFORE EIGHT HOURS OF
UNINTERRUPTED COMATOSE SLEEP IS EVER EXPERIENCED AGAIN.

AND THEN THERE'S MY BUST LINE, MAKE THAT... WHAT BUST LINE?
I BREAST FED. THIRTY SIX "C" BEFORE, THIRTY TWO "A" AFTER.
NO FURTHER COMMENTS.

THAT CRISP CLEAN MILITARY LOOK THAT I ONCE DONNED BEFORE LEAVING HOME IS ALSO A
JUST A THOUGHT, A MEMORY. IT'S BEEN REPLACED BY A FEW CRUSTED OVER STAINS ON MY
FAVORITE SUIT, DRIED PUREED SQUASH ON MY LUCKY SWEATER AND SOME MURKY STUFF
THAT BLENDS IN WITH MY FLOWERED SHIRT FROM MARSHALS. DID I SAY MARSHALS?
YES, I SAID MARSHALS.

IF YOU THINK THIS CAN'T HAPPEN TO YOU. THINK AGAIN.
FIRST YOUR PRIDE WILL DIE, THEN SLOWLY, MINUTE BY MINUTE YOU WILL DIE TOO AND ALL
THE WHILE YOUR TODDLER'S LAUGHING, PLAYING, SPITTING ON YOU, PUKING ON YOU AND
REQUIRING THAT YOU BUILD A FIRST HAND RELATIONSHIP WITH THE STENCH OF TWO
THOUSAND SOILED DIAPERS. I KNOW WHY GOD MADE BABY POOP SMELL SO BAD; IT'S SO
THAT YOU'D HAVE TO GET UP AND CHANGE THEM IMMEDIATELY INSTEAD OF WAITING
A COUPLE OF DAYS.

WORKING OUT, TEN PERFECT NAILS AND TOES: GONE. EVERY STRAND IN PLACE BEFORE EVEN
THINKING ABOUT LEAVING THE HOUSE; GONE. THE ORGANIZED CLOSET: GONE. THE SPRING
CLEANING THAT TAKES PLACE EVERY SPRING, FORGET IT HONEY: GONE.

SIXTY MINUTES, THE MORNING PAPER, THE SOCIETY PAGE: GONE. IT'S PUBLIC TELEVISION
AND DISNEY VIDEOS SO NO HARD QUESTIONS OKAY?

I'M A MURDER VICTIM, REMEMBER?

THERE'S A CHANCE THAT I MAY ESCAPE THIS TODDLERISM WITH MY LIFE AND JUST IN CASE
I DO, THE EXPERTS TELL ME I'VE GOT JUST ENOUGH TIME TO START SAVING UP FOR COLLEGE.

HAVING KIDS IS GOD'S WAY OF PUNISHING YOU FOR KNOWING WHAT TO DO WITH
EVERYBODY ELSE'S CHILDREN, BEFORE YOU HAD YOUR OWN.

No Apologies

Today is the day that I stop being sorry for all the things that I've been sorry about.

I've been sorry for misunderstanding, sorry for understanding, sorry for wanting

to be understood. I've been sorry for you, sorry for me and so sorry so many times.

But it's all good, all of those sorries have built a cradle for a sorry me that's just

too sorry to continue in the same sorry way. So it is with all the love and care for

the universe that I give my sorries to the forlorn female in the misty azure shade.

I write myself a bill of freedom with a decree to simply be. And as the sorries

sail into oblivion, I can exhale and breathe again for all the yesterdays that I cried

my beloved soul away, my groove is back to life, back to a new reality, there's no

more rain in this cloud. I don't mind company because company is all right

with me. You see there's a new Dr. Feelgood and the doctor is a she. The doctor

is me and she has kicked sorry to the curb permanently. Yes I exist imperfectly.

Errors are politely addressed, courtesies are graciously extended but

as for me being me, there are no more apologies.

CALLING FORTH BOOM SHENANA SHAY SHAY

I don't know why they choose to beckon her. She's perfectly fine sleeping, resting, hiding, going virtually unnoticed beneath crispy cool exteriors, sultry sophistication or humble holiness. But then someone, some unsuspecting fool decides to "go there" and for some unknown reason they keep on going. Pushing the envelope, pressing the issue and going in high gear on the panic button until they become totally unglued allowing all forms of nastiness and negativity to spew from their filthy mouths straight at the human cage that shelters the almighty Boom Shannon Shay who hails from the planet Bitchatoria!

'What did you say mother f'er, I will kick your ass. You don't know who the hell you're dealing with!'

Oh my God, she has spoken! She received an invitation and she has shown up to the party in vivid colors.

'I don't give a damn about your ass. See you don't know me, like you think you know me!'

And so the filthy exchange begins.

Now you see, it is just as well that no one knows of Boom Shenana Shay Shay. She would rather be a mystery that lives loudly but only in the subconscious mind that isn't afraid of being judged.

In the real world, Boom Shenana Shay Shay is just a thin line away from being in someone's face just moments after they have breached the realm of mutual respect. Boom Shenana Shay Shay is also channeled quite frequently on city streets and highways, specially during rush hour.

'Get out of my way, ass hole! Hey! You cut me off!! Learn how to drive stupid!
Don't make me have to get out of this car!!

With the flip of a carefully selected finger, Boom Shenana Shay Shay has spoken and sped off.

Finally, to the unsuspecting public, I say leave Shay Shay alone. Let her masquerade in perfect composure and sanctity. Let her take cover in polite posture and anonymity. Again I say, leave that woman alone! Boom Shenana Shay Shay/ Boom Shenana Shay Shay is just a neck roll away. When boom Shenana Shay Shay speaks, it's embarrassing for she gives you a reading fit for all past life experiences. There may be pain but there is no shame with Boom Shenana Shay Shay. So leave her be and let her eternally rest in the land of Bitchatoria where there are no ulcers, migraines, fibroids or hemorrhoids. Boom Shenana Shay Shay, Boom Shenana Shay Shay, Boom Shenana Shay Shay!

READING AND CHECKING

I spent the whole day reading & checking
and reading & checking
and reading & reading
check, check, check!

A friend pissed me off so I read her and checked her,
I read her, I checked her
I told her, I scolded her
I got to the point

My brother mad me mad so I read him, I checked him
I read him, I checked him
I got in his face, I put him in place

This girl where I work, had worked my last nerve
so the reading was on, the checking was on
Yes I read her, I checked her
I read her, I checked her
She was so incorrect with her lack of respect

Then one day I was needing
the comfort of a friend
and I thought of who hadn't
annoyed me in some way
who could live up to my standard
of a perfect person and friend
who hadn't been read
who hadn't been checked
who hadn't been served
whose feelings had I preserved
while reading & checking
and reading & checking

who did I trust enough to read me
and when was the last time I read myself
and who had appointed me the chief librarian anyway?
If I spent as much time reading myself
I wouldn't have so much time left
for reading and checking,
reading and checking,
reading and checking,
check please!

For Men

THE LATITUDES OF ATTITUDES/ MALE VERSION
(Can be done by one or more actors)

What he said was: "You better get out of my face 'cause you don't know what the f*ck you're talking about!!"

But what he meant was: "Baby, now is not the time, for whatever reason I can't hear you.
Right now, is not the time."

What he said was: "I don't need you do so if you don't like what I'm putting down, you can pack your sh*t
and get the hell up out of here."

But what he meant was: "Baby I got more questions than answers running through my head right now.
I'm trying to figure this thing out. So just in case I don't get my sh*t together in time,
you are free to go.

What he said was: "All you ever talk about is what you did, you did this and you did that. And you're always
bringing sh*t up from the past."

But what he meant was: "You remind me of my worst moments. You bring your list of good things
to me and it angers me because my list is not as long or as perfect as yours but I am
loving you the best way I know how."

What he said was: 'I shouldn't have never been with you in the first place, you're nothing like I thought!
Living with you is hell! You go against everything I say!

But what he meant was: I have a difficult time accepting you and trusting you because society
has made it difficult for me to trust myself. I have to make you my enemy because I've been trained
to question anything too good to be true and woman, you are too good to be true.

What he said was: ".....F'in' bitch.
But what he meant was: You can see me like no one else sees me. I am completely uncovered
before you and that's a difficult place for a man to be in. I was taught to fight, to hunt, to kill
and to protect. It is my nature and now you're judging me for my unbridled male instinct!
It just may be easier for you to leave me than to love me. It may be easier for me to hurt
you than to accept you because then I would have to learn how to love you and I'm still learning
how to love myself.

THE LATITUDES OF ATTITUDES

IT'S IN MY WALK

They watch me, they ask me why my stroll my saunter is so proud, so different, so laid back and so lanky. They see me move and they can't resist the rhythm of my motion. And I say hey, I can't help this soulful saunter. It's who I am, a black man and it's in my walk.

My truth is in my walk, my history, my flow. Weather I am in a designer suit or sporting baggy pants with laced up Jordans, the universe has allowed me a fluent method of foot transportation and it's in my walk. It's in the walk that Denzil had when he coasted up the hill in The Preacher's Wife. It's the walk of Sam Jackson, Will Smith or some other brother in your neighborhood.

This walk is confident, it's secure and seductive and it can charm the panties off of a teenage virgin. It can also make an old woman remember the last time she had a tremble somewhere beneath her navel and above her thighs. I've got a good dose of it. That certain something and it's in my walk.

It's in the walk of Jay Z and Master P when they sluggishly stroll onto the stage to accept an accolade and like I said before I got it too. It's in my walk. I'm a black man and I've got to walk differently because the roads that I have traveled have been paved differently. It's the walk that occurs after being pulled over by a friendly law enforcement officer. You get out of the car, sit on the sidewalk and wait for your license and vehicle to be checked. Upon finding out that everything is all right, a quick shake of the jacket launches into a confident stride that rekindles the momentary loss of dignity. It's the walk that fits the profile, it's the walk that commands and demands. It's the walk that says I don't give a damn and it's the walk that says I care. It's the walk of Jesse, Wesley, General Powell and Puffy Daddy. It's the walk of Sgt. Jones, Coach Brown and even my daddy. So don't be perplexed by the rhythm of my stroll. What you see is the celebration of my soul, I'm a black man and the victory is in my walk!

ANGRY BLACK MAN'S POEM
(This piece is intended to be a bit of a farce. It is a satire of all the angry black man's poems and depictions)

Whatcha lookin' at? Huh? You lookin' at me? Cause if you ARE looking at ME then I might not

LIKE the way that you're LOOKING at me cause' then I'd have to ask you WHY you're looking at me in the first

place? So what's your problem? Cause, see it must be a problem with YOU cuss I ain't GOT no problem up in

here. See, I know you. You're part of that man's system, see. And that system is designed to keep a brother on

the bus stop so when the car pulls up to the stop sign he will know that the car (that is, the AUTOMOBILE) is

NOT for him but for the white devil and all of their good credit and all of that buuuull shit.

Yeah, yeah See, that's just how they did Malcom. In fact that's how they did Malcom, Michael

Jordan and Michael Jackson. But they will not steal my other shiny glove!

I vacuum, I wash my plate and all and I'm a good man around the house.

I, yes I the black king, the original man must reign! The chains of oppression and brutality still mark

my bloody soul! And what did Soul Train do for the black race? And where are the Lockers? What happened

to the original pop lockers? I'm telling you America it's all part of the plan to destroy the Zulu God.

I must be strong, I must be armed at all times to defend myself, to defend the Black Nation because it's the

BLACK WOMAN'S FAULT. She's the one that's behind all of this. See, she got a PROBLEM. She's driving

Lexusis, wearing gold changes and getting her hair all done up in those fancy styles. See she's either going to

the beauty shop with her own magazine or finding one when she gets there. Then she's asking the beautician

to make her look like the woman in the book and y'all know that ain't right! She's reading all of those

articles AND she's been listening to Oprah and that other woman whose name I can't pronounce. Evonda,

Iyanda or something like that. Hell, that black woman is so screwed up she don't want to hear NOTHING I say.

And I've been to school, the school of the streets, the school of the sheets and the school of MR. CHARLIE!

But that man, his system and his Billy club will never tie me down. The Zulu God must reign and I will never

give up my DOO RAG or my can of DUKE for I wear the ROYAL CROWN and I shall forever grip

the Holy Grail of Johnny Walker until they entomb my ebony carcass tightly clinching the fist of an Afro

pick, a brand new black man's shaver and a bronze bust of O.J. Simpson.

SHE BROUGHT GREAT DRAMA

I knew it! I knew the woman was trouble when she asked me if my shirt was one hundred percent silk on our first date. At the end of our stormy affair she slit my tires, cracked my windshield and burned half my clothes. In short she brought great drama and her show had to be canceled. All right, I'll level with you sometimes I'm not the easiest guy to get along with and I did have a few ladies on the side.
I'm a popular guy and I happen to meet a lot of women. There's no sin in testing the waters. What most women don't understand is that commitment is a monumental step for most brothers. It's not like we're all looking to be dogs, it's just that settling down does not bear the same immediate importance for our gender. Eventually most of us get there but it's not like one day we just wake up and say "Okay, today is the today is the day that I'm going to say no to all of the punanny in the world because I've got this great woman who wants me to be hers forever!" Like I said, eventually we get there but we don't jump for the golden ring of commitment all at once. The other odd thing about us is that the one woman who we usually settle down with is the one who's survived the most bullshit with grace and style. Anyway back to my story about Miss Drama, this woman really had it going on. Yes, she caught me in a lie but instead of playing it cool she went to the farthest degree of crazy paranoia. She became the star sixty nine queen, she followed me, she called my other lady friends, she came to my job, she called my mother and vandalized my belongings. I know men can be stupid sometimes. Sometimes we can mess up a good thing by being greedy or by thinking that we can fool somebody when it's obvious that we're cheating? What Miss Drama failed to realize is that I've messed up before but there are women who I will always respect, maybe come back and marry because of how they handled themselves even when my interpersonal dealings were less than desirable.

A calm and collected woman who deals with the mental to bring about a change in the physical and emotional is probably the one woman to put my stuff in check and cause me to turn completely around. But hey I'm not rushing to be an altar boy, either. As for the empress of dramatic tactics. This femme fatale took one cue to bring on the drama, thinking that would make me change. She thought that by seeking revenge I would instantly associate my actions as the source of feelings of hurt or betrayal. Ump, her actions only made me dislike her and even though I was wrong, I felt like I was now the victim of a crazy woman. She brought drama, *great* drama and therefore her show had to be canceled.

HOOK A BROTHER (HOMIE) UP

Hey man, you got the hook up? Now come on, I KNOW you got the hook up cause if anybody's got the hook up, it's got to be you! Come on man, get me in, give me a deal, break, a discount, a cut back, a pass, a voucher... anything but the full price. You know I can't pay that man, cause I'm a brother that needs the hook up! Maybe not always, but right about now, that's what time it is! Can you hook me up? Can you cut me some slack, give me some lead way, let me slide I don't care how you do it just hook me up! You know me man, my first question ain't never gonna be "How much does it cost?" My first question is always gonna be "Can you give the brother the hook up?" That's right, The Hook UP! The first class ticket for the price of coach, the best bottle of champagne for the price of a beer, the tune up, new engine and brake job for the cost of an oil change or better yet FREE! I want the hook up, I need the hook up so come on.... HOOK A BROTHER UP!

CAUGHT

It seemed like it would have been the easiest thing in the world. All I had to do was admit that I was wrong, apologize and then see what the next phase would be. Why did this seem so difficult? Why did I now want to fight?

"Look, just worry about me and you okay! Just focus on the now! Just stick to dealing with me and you all right?"

I was covering. It wasn't the noblest way out but I was covering my own embarrassment with more and more anger and more and more defensiveness.

"Now wait a minute baby, we're not married yet, I have friends and this is my house! That thing could belong to anybody! Don't you have visitors to your house?"

I can't explain it but I felt backed into a corner. I'm usually so on top of my game. How did I let this tiny piece of evidence miss being discarded and more importantly, when did I grant this person the right to give me the third degree?

"What? When I slept with you? Are you saying that because I slept with you, you now have to know every damn thing that goes on in my whole life? Hell you slept with me too. Do I come over your house snooping in your trash cans? When I throw something in the garbage I just throw it in. I don't look to see what else is in there already! See, you have a problem with insecurity, that's what's wrong with you."

Good move. The bait was taken. We're into round two.

"That's right you're insecure, immature and you over reacting!. You are so typical!"

My opponent is now in second gear on the defense! I have diverted the original subject matter of my cheating by suggesting the character flaws of my accuser. The tone of the argument is now a series of personal attacks. The anger is rising and more insults will hurl. This alone will stir up enough strife between us and we will strategically turn our attention to the things that we dislike about each other. This will also build up enough surface resentment so that I will have an opportunity to end the relationship and I'll never, ever have to deal with my own personal issue. The fact is that I was irresponsible and I was caught. I lied. I said we were monogamous and I just plain lied.

HE JUST WASN'T

Man I used to sit and wonder what it would be like to take a walk with my dad and ask him all kinds of questions like: 'Dad, when did you first start liking girls? or when did you have your first wet dream or when was the first time that a girl let you kiss her?' Usually it was questions like that because face it, there's just some things you can't discuss with your mother. I would want to know if my dad's mom ever caught him with his hands underneath the cover and if he'd quickly roll on his side and tried to play it off like I did. I wondered if pop's ever found a safer place for his teenage magazines than between the mattress because for some reason, that's the first place mom tends to look. As I got a little older, it was all about my dad seeing me handle things on the court or actually winning an award for academic achievement. I used to see some of my boys kicking it with their pops and I'd cop a position like I didn't even care, like I didn't even notice that they had something that I always wanted. My mom says that he just stopped coming around one day. I don't think they were ever married and I don't know if he's got another family or not. As far as I know it wasn't even about money. My mother worked hard and I never wanted for anything that she could provide but to be honest, to be totally honest... I did okay for myself but I always wanted my dad around and he wasn't... he just wasn't.

HE WAS BUT I WISH HE WASN'T

I dreaded the moment he hit the door. If I somehow missed getting into a fight out on the streets then for damn sure I had a fight on my hands when I got home... not with my sisters, not with my brother or my mother but with my father. Can you even imagine what it feels like to be loved and hated equally by a man that hates himself? It was some hard and strange kind of love in that house. Shoot, brother's aren't known for sharing but this is some truth that I have tried to drink away, drug away, sex away and pray away. This is some truth that I still don't know how to sort out. There is no suit expensive enough to disguise this anguish for long and there is no woman that I can penetrate deep enough to make me remember who I really was before I was told that I was nothing by the very man whose sperm created me. When this man finally dies, I don't even know if I'll feel remorse or relief. Yeah, my father was around. He was around every day and night. He was there, he was right there. He was, but I wish he wasn't.

HE WAS AND I'M GLAD HE WAS

I would be lost if it weren't for my Pops. For as long as I can remember he was there racing me, boxing me, channeling me and calling me his Champ. 'Seems like nothing happened until Pops came home. We couldn't eat until Pops came home. If one of us had to go to the doctor or the dentist, we couldn't until Pops came home. If one of us got in trouble, boy it was on when Pops came home. If we got good grades we'd all get a big Pizza or a box of donuts when Pops came home. If he and my moms ever did fuss and fight, they never did it when we were around. Pops wasn't even much of a talker, he didn't even show that much emotion towards us, we just knew that he brought a strong sense of security to our household. If we ever had a problem, we could talk to Pops. He'd listen to our hour long interpretation of whatever the situation was and then Pop's would come up with an answer in just one simple sentence that was more profound than the three pages of dialogue that it took us to discuss the problem in the first place. He let my mom be the queen of her castle, though that was no easy task with all of us bad kids running around. Pops wasn't a complicated man, he didn't need a lot of fancy things. We were the ones always running around needing this and that. Most of the time, we got everything we requested. Pops was there for us. He was and I'm glad he was.

THE PROMOTION

"Darren, I want you to know how much you mean to this company and I really appreciate all of your hard work." That's where the conversation ended with Bruce Weinstien as I shut off my cell phone upon entering the parking garage at our regional headquarters early that Friday morning. Company reps were parking all makes and models of expensive cars and SUV's and delegates were filing in from all over the tri-state area.

I felt especially proud, having a five year tenure with the company and having moved up the ranks as swiftly as I did to make National Sales Manager in a very short time. I was also pleased to have earned my status purely based on my efforts and not on race. Who could ignore the huge drop in minority hires after the reversal of Affirmative Action? I was convinced that my contributions to this company would be color blind and they were. The campaign, which I master minded and took to Bruce Weinstein was the key to the eighty percent increase in revenue which our company has seen over the last three quarters. I was also very happy with Bruce's decision to accept my recommendations to cut company spending on international shipping and shift the residual budget over to domestic marketing. I was filled with the pride of a man who had finally proven himself. The nights out for drinks, the Saturday's on the Golf Course and all the Sunday dinners that I missed with my family had paid off.

I entered the assembly hall and assumed my seat at the head table. I looked across a sea of white shirts, dark suits and white faces. As soon as I was Vice President, I would look into the company's current status on the diversity issue. I wouldn't rock the boat too much but I would at least check into it.

After a few moments of hand shakes and small talk the usual formalities were underway. Bruce presided over the meeting: "I'd like to thank you all for coming out this morning. As you know our Industry has experience a favorable turn around over the past year and I'd like to thank Darrin Johnson for working so diligently with me to come up with a solution for our corporation." Now I thought; 'What does he mean working *with* him, the whole campaign was my idea?' It was probably just my nerves getting the best of me. Then he continued. "We needed to increase our profits, reduce our spending and reposition ourselves ahead of our competitors and that's just what we did. I spent countless hours going over proposals, analyzing spread sheets and working with our branch managers to execute precisely where the residual spending would pay off most. This company came up with a solution. No one man is greater than the company itself but there is one man who stands a cut above today..."

As Bruce went on, I admit I was a little put off by his opening banter about *the company* coming up with the solution but the butterflies in my stomach were about to give way to the shear excitement of accepting my promotion. Bruce paused and then continued. He always had a flair for the dramatic. "There is one man who stands a cut above today. I have pushed him to the limits. We have worked hard many days, nights and weekends together. We have laughed, we have fought and we've have more than a few rounds of indigestion from ordering late night fast food. I believe that he truly represents the future of this company and it is my honor to appoint him as Vice President of National Sales and Marketing and he is.... my son Brian Weinstein."

WHAT! *Brian?* He's only a kid... he worked as my gofer! He doesn't have half the skills I do! (sotto) 'Careful Darrin, you are at the head table, look happy.... get on your feet and clap like everyone else.

I had to stand up and salute my new boss, who I trained, whose salary I created when I helped this company grow! Bruce took his seat back at the table and shot me a quirky grin with the thumbs up, he leaned in and whispered towards me. "We got special things in store for you Darren, we couldn't have done this without you."

As the meeting ended and everyone rushed to congratulate the new V.P. I thought about what I would say to Bruce's son... and then I thought about what I would tell my own son on that day... the day of the great Promotion!

SHE WANTED ME TO MISS THE GAME

For the past few months I've been kicking it with a honey that is so fine, she'd make a brother want to throw away his black book. She's so fine she'd make a brother want to think about settling down and makin' a few little shorties of his own. This woman was the shiz...met!

Now I admit that I'd been checking her out for a while and she'd been checking me out too, so quite naturally when we got the chance to hook up there was some serious bonding goin' on. And when we got to *hit it!* I mean, man it was *off the chain!* That sister's got some sweet stuff. I mean this woman could be the one.... *SHE* could be my Boo!

We ended up spending a lot of time together cause she was so cool to kick back with. I mean it was *almost* like being with one of my boys, except my boys can't cook or put me in a leg lock like she can. Well after a few blissful months, my baby said to me, "Honey, my sister and my best friend are coming to town next Sunday and you've just got to meet them."

Sure babe, was my immediate reply. You see this was my new lady and I didn't mind meeting her peeps. "They're only going to be here for a few hours, they've got a lay over, so I thought we'd drive to the airport and hang out with them for a while." That's what my baby said and it seemed like a cool idea. 'What time are they arriving,' I asked with every good intention. "Three o'clock," she said. *'Three O'clock?'* "Yeah baby, three o'clock." *Three o'clock in the afternoon next Sunday?'* "Yes Charles, Three O'clock in the afternoon next Sunday." You mean, your best friend and your sister are coming to town *next* Sunday at *three o'clock?'*

"Is there a problem? Is there something I don't know about? One minute you're down with going to the airport to meet my folks and the next minute you're questioning me like there's something wrong, like you don't wanna even meet my sister. Is there a *problem* Charles?"

Now I knew I'd better do some explaining fast because my baby was about to spin into a neck roll and her hand was headed straight for her hip. 'Uhm, that's the game baby... ah next Sunday at three o'clock... the... the game is on.' There! I said it and she replied, "Oh sweetie, is that all. We can tape the game." 'NO, we can't. I mean we *can* but... I *can't*. I can't miss this one. I mean I gotta be there live, not *really* live like *being at the game* in person but live, like *while* the game is going on!' Suddenly I felt the mood start to change so I put on a boyish grin and echoed . 'Do you understand baby?'

Yeah so now I was pleading like Lenny Williams, Keith Sweat and Boyz II Men combined but I had to be smart. Now the big game *may* have been next week but *I* was horny as hell *tonight!* I had to handle this situation with care.

"Charles, do you mean to tell me that you can't miss one little old game for the sake of meeting my sister and my best friend? You have got to be kidding. You can watch the game at the airport or listen to it on the radio!"

Woa, woa, woa.. wait up. A dose of reality was starting to set in. Did she say watch the game at the airport or listen to it on the radio? Was this the woman I was thinking about spending the rest of my life with? Naw, this woman didn't really know me at all! This was a point of serious reckoning because the thought of meeting her folks in *no way* compared to me witnessing first hand the most anticipated athletic event since the beginning of the current basketball season. She wasn't feelin' my pain at all. She wanted *me* to *miss the game!*

If she thought for a *minute* that I'd miss a *second* of the game of the season then she was surely mistaken. This was no *ordinary* basketball game. This was the two top scorers in the NBA squaring off for the first time!! Shoot just walking through the terminal alone may cause me to be absent or late for the thrill of victory or the agony of defeat!! This was history!!!

And taping it? Did she say that I should just TAPE it? All of my boys are gonna be calling me to see if *I'm* side line coaching like *they* are. This woman was *wrong*, she was *raw,* she was *out of control,* she was selfish... man, she wanted me to miss the game! She wanted ME to miss the game! The GAME, ...THE game!!!! And just think... She could've been my Boo!

SHE WAS ALL OVER ME

She was all over me
but I wasn't feeling her

She was tall, she was sweet
but I could not concur

So she smiled and suggested
I politely protested

She was wild, she was free
she was all over me

She wanted to be near me
and to know me from the heart

She thought that she could steer me
to a movie or the park

Her advance was complimentary
but she began to cross the line

My cordial style of rejection
was running out of time

Miss, you're making me uncomfortable
what you see is not what you get

I have nothing for you
but a sea of regret

You're coming on too strong
as your desperation shows

I'm not up for grabs
and please don't touch my clothes

I would like to bow out gracefully
without the need to reveal

That *your* type isn't *my* type
and I'm not swayed by your sex appeal

I am who I am
and what I do is my business to keep
but it was like talking to the wind
still, she was all over me.

IDENTITY

For all the energy and effort that I put into being me, I have to question myself sometimes as to who I really am. Am I my job, my clothes or my car? Am I a set of numbers on a paycheck or am I best described by a few Latin words on my diploma. Is it my family that has given me my identity? Have I become who I thought they wanted me to become or did I intentionally defy their direction to come up with some new and unique person that they despise? Have I become the person that I most despise?

Is my identity in my name? Is it in my father's name or my family name? Is it in history books, billboards or sports magazines that most identifies the man that I am? And what about my woman? Does a certain type of woman automatically fit my assumed persona? What kind of woman makes me feel secure? What does she look like? How does she smell? What does she do and how does she do it that determines that this is where my time, energy and possibly my money will be spent?

In what spiritual force do I identify? Is there some Godly image or deity that hits me in the pit of my stomach with the certainty that I have found strength, wisdom, and understanding?

Could I still be me if I wore different clothes? If I had to live on a different side of town or thrive on an income that is the polar opposite of what I have now? Could I survive being the one and only of my kind in a corporation, a neighborhood, a city or even a nation? What if I woke up one morning and everyone... and everything that validated or supported this supposed identity of mine was gone? Would I still be me, would I still have an identity? Would I change to be like everyone else or what if everyone was exactly the same, would I even have an identity at all?

The Plays

ESPRESSO CAFE

Dramatic One Act

2 characters (can be all male or female or mixed cast)

*Max- 20-40   The manager of the local coffee shop. Good natured & can
be surprisingly strong.*

P.J.- 25-35   A little strange, a little tentative but can be a time bomb if prompted.

*Setting: Any town USA, an autumn morning. P.J. comes in for the usual late but
today something is not quite right.*

ESPRESSO CAFE:
Max is tending the counter when P.J. enters.

P.J.:   'Morning Max.

Max: Good morning P.J.,

P.J.:   I'll have a...

Max: I know, you'll have a late with an apple bran muffin. You always
have the same thing everyday P.J.

P.J.:   I know Max. 'Guess I'm just a creature of habit. (beat) Did anyone come
here looking for me yesterday?

Max: Hum, no. Not that I know of. Maybe I could ask some of the others.

P.J.:   No. That won't be necessary. (tastes the muffin) There's too much bran
in this muffin. It's supposed to be an apple bran muffin and all I taste is bran.

Max: Hey I'm sorry P.J., would you like to try another one? We wouldn't want you
to miss out on getting your fiber on the account that there's not enough apple
in it.

P.J.:   Are you making fun of me?

Max: No, you're my buddy. 'Besides I've been sniffing coffee beans all day what
do I know? I wonder where in the world is Taylor? She's usually here by now.

P.J.:   I don't think she's coming today?

Max: Now P.J., you come here often but how are you gone know my employees better than I do?

P.J.:   I just don't think she's coming that's all. (sips coffee) Boy this coffee sure is extra good today.

Max: Thanks buddy, since we didn't suit your fancy on the muffin, I'm glad the coffee is to your satisfaction. Excuse me for a minute. (goes to the phone. After a few rings, the answering machine picks up.) Hi Taylor, this is Max. Are you coming in today? Where are you? Give me a ring okay. Bye now.

P.J.:   Can I have some more coffee?

Max: Are you sure you have time? You're usually the first one in after we unlock the doors and long gone before the next customer strolls in.

P.J.:   (blankly) I've got time. Can I have some more coffee?

Max: Coffee you want. Coffee you got. Here you are. (beat) Boy I'm starting to get worried about Taylor. This is not like her at all.

P.J.:   Taylor didn't treat me nice yesterday.

Max: What? Come again?

P.J.:   Taylor didn't put enough foam in my late?

Max: Now P.J. aren't you being a little, well.... a little too picky?

P.J.:   (a slight chuckle) I guess I am, it's no wonder no one wants to be bothered with me.

Max: AHD, I'm sure it's not that bad, there's always your family. By the way, where's yours?

P.J.:   They're all dead, the immediate ones anyway. What little I got left are back in Oregon.

Max: Well how did they....

P.J.: *It was something terrible, they never caught the guy. One day I just came home from work and they were just gone. (takes out a picture) Two little girls and one perfect soul mate... gone in a flash.*

Max: *You know I'd really like to know more but only if you feel like talking about it. (beat) I had a tragedy to happen to me once. My best friend was murdered, some whack was actually trying to set up one of my family members and ended up killing my friend instead and... AHD, here I am rattling on. What difference does it make? How you making out?*

P.J.: *You know what makes me upset by it all?*

Max: *What's that?*

P.J.: *It's how they always somehow suspect you, like you had something to do with it!*

Max: *I'm not sure I'm with you on that.*

P.J.: *(obviously on a tangent) First they want to know how things were going in the relationship, if you were happy or had been fighting, then they want to know when you last saw the person or what time you left from work, if you had an alibi or if you'd taken out any insurance lately....*

Max: *But Max there had to be some reason for them to suspect you don't you think? Hey, I'm not saying that what happened was....*

P.J.: *(outburst) What the hell do you know about it? Now you're questioning me! Who the hell do you think you are to be questioning me?*

Max: *Well... I....*

P.J.: *Well I nothing! Shut up and pour the damn coffee cause ain't nobody leaving here right now. (He storms toward the door locks it, goes to his briefcase and clutches it tightly to his chest).*

Max: *P.J., P.J. It's all right buddy, just calm down. Look is it money you need? What is it P.J.? This isn't like you....*

P.J.   "Like" me, what do you mean this isn't "like" me. You don't even know me!
          'You think you know a person 'cause you have a cup of coffee with 'em?
          You dumb ass! You'll be working here a long time, if they don't recruit
          you for a corn dog stand. This is reality baby, and in reality you don't
          really know anybody. You don't know the person you work with, sleep with
          or the person who's driving the car next to you! (smells something funny)
          What is it? What is that?

Max: It's, it's nothing... it's... are you talking about the coffee?

P.J.:   Yes, what is it? It's making me sick!!

Max: It's just a new Colombian brew, we got it in this morning.

P.J.:   Take it off, pour it out or burn it. I don't care what you do with it,
          just get rid of that awful smell!!

Max: (deciding to take a different stance) Wait a minute, now just wait a minute!
          I'm working here! I belong here! You, my friend have obviously got something
          bugging you and what ever it is, it's not me, it's not this coffee shop and going
          on a rampage will only make your problems worse! Now you make one more
          move towards me and I'm calling the police!!

P.J.:   (taken aback but a bit amused) Ohh, okay. (thinks a moment) Okay.
          (beat) So where do I get the nerve to collect myself here and realize that
          I've just gone completely off the deep end?

Max: Just relax P.J., just relax. (slowly) I'm unlocking the door.(checking with PJ)
          We're okay now aren't we? (goes to discard the Colombian coffee.)

P.J.:   (slowly putting down his briefcase) Max, I need another cup of coffee.
          'Better make this one decaf.

Max: (Max notices something bulging out of the briefcase but does not let
          PJ know that he has seen it.) I will get you some help P.J. but we've got to go
          about this the right way.

P.J.:   I miss my family Max. I miss them and there's not one thing I can do about it.

Max: Go on

P.J.:   *We were living in a town just outside of Cuba. I had my days of being a runner, a drug runner and I wanted to get out and start my own business. I wanted to come clean so that I wouldn't have to worry about my safety and the safety of my family. I always had a love for cars and even though I was never any good with fixing cars, I wanted to run an auto shop. That's what my father did so I guess I wanted to carry out the family tradition.*

Max: *Wait a minute, you used to run an auto shop?*

P.J.:   *I sure did. I borrowed the money from my former client or boss whatever you wanna call him. It was actually a family of them, the Santiagos from Columbia.*

Max: *(has a moment of recognition but tries to hide it.) The Santiagos?*

P.J.:   *Yeah, nice people... if you want to live a life of crime, I can't think of a better family. Well they loaned me the money and I renovated a two story garage. My family and I lived in the top story and the first floor was where I ran the business. It was going great and in less than a year I paid off my loan but that wasn't good enough. My former associates wanted to use my shop to remake stolen vehicles, first one, then another and then another. I went along with it at first just to keep the peace but then I was right back in the life again, and...*

Max: *...and that's the reason you got out in the first place.*

P.J.:   *Right... so I wouldn't be looking over my shoulder all of the time. Hey I'm a good person, I just needed money from time to time. Well I finally refused to service or deface any more stolen property! That was it, I was not gonna do it! (long beat) For the next couple of weeks, everything was fine but I had a funny feeling that it wasn't gonna be over just like that. It was two days before the New Year and the shop closed early because we were going out of town for the holiday. My family was upstairs packing and preparing for the trip. I had to run an errand farther into the city, so after we closed up. I took off. I was only gone for an hour but when I returned my whole shop was in flames, my family, my business, my whole life up in smoke. I did everything they asked me to do up until the point where I wanted to come clean. All I wanted was to come clean!! I swear that I will hate the Santiagos as long as I live!*

Max: *The Santiagos? So you worked for the Santiago family?*

P.J.:   *Wake up and smell the f#%*ing coffee Max. The Santiagos are now in the coffee business which they used all along as a front for their cocaine smuggling. Importing coffee was a logical choice because it dilutes any strong scent. If it's a huge cargo of coffee beans then not too much else can be sniffed out get my drift. Now everybody is into having their 'designer' coffees so why not open a string of coffee shops as sort of an expansion of the family business?*

Max: (with rising suspicion) Why have you shown up here everyday and why have
          you been here asking questions for the last two months come to think of it.

(there is an awkward beat)

P.J.:   How much do you know about the Santiago family Max?

Max: Well, ah...

P.J.:   Cut the crap and tell me how much you know?

(Max reaches beneath the counter as if going for supplies and pulls out a
 surprise weapon)

Max: Stay away from my family! You're not doing this again!

(completely taken aback)

P.J.:   Stay away from your family?!! What do you mean stay away from
          your family? Are you one of them?

(Max doesn't answer)

P.J.:   I said are you one of them?!!!

Max: I am and I had nothing to do with what happened to your family!

(Now P.J. reaches from a secret pocket and pulls another weapon. It's a stand off)

P.J.:   Well how do I know that? I'll never trust a Santiago again as long as I
          live and as long as I live, I plan to stop at nothing until I see that every one
          of them is either dead or behind bars.

Max: Where's my sister?

P.J.:   (with surprise) Sister? Taylor was your sister?

Max: What do you mean was? She's innocent and had nothing to do with it!

P.J.:   Just like my wonderful spouse and kids had nothing to do with the
          Santiago family but where are they now?

Max: I'm sorry for what happened to your family but if you've hurt my sister
       I swear I'll blow your brains all over this coffee shop!.

P.J.: (now clutching his briefcase) You do it, I'm as good as dead anyway!

Max: What's in the briefcase!

P.J.: It's nothing.

Max: That's bull sh*t, P.J. what did you do when you found out that
       the Santiago's had killed your family?

P.J.: (no response)

Max: I'll tell you what you did. You went back to your home town. You somehow
       managed a disguise and staked out some more distant members of the Santiago
       family. You ended up kidnapping and killing a girl that you 'thought' was the
       niece of Juan Carlo Santiago but you got the wrong girl P.J. The girl you thought
       was Patrina Santiago was a girl who had just finished college and she was a
       second cousin to the Santiagos. Her name was Anita, she was completely
       innocent and she was my best friend. (real choked up). She never hurt nobody.

P.J.: You're wrong....

Max: Shut up you bastard! Where's Taylor?

P.J.: I should be asking you. You're in charge here aren't you?

Max: Where's Taylor? She's late to work PJ and she has never been late before!!!

(P.J.: withdraws the weapon, lays it on a table and goes over and sits in a corner
       and begins to whistle a lullaby)

Max: (puzzled) What? What are you doing?

P.J.: I'm whistling, what does it look like I'm doing?

Max: I'll kill you, you know that?

P.J.: Yeah sure. If you were a killer, you would have killed me already.

Max: (more and more angry) Stop playing games P.J. This is my family we're
       talking about here!

P.J.:   *(not phased by Max's outburst) You know what Max, I'm an early riser and I've been here for a few minutes now. I'd say in about a half hour or less your usual crew of customers are gonna come barging through these doors for their morning fix. So if you're gonna shoot me, go ahead and shoot me. What do ya say? I'm lying here in a pool of blood dead as road kill and it don't look too good for you, now does it?*

Max: *Stop playing mind games rookie...*

P.J.:   *What would it be self defense? No, now that wouldn't go over too well because my weapon is all the way over there. How about a crime of passion because you thought I killed Taylor when I really didn't kill her, she's just late for work. Well what do you know (opens the briefcase) I happen to have her uniform in my briefcase or is it one that just looks like hers.*

(with that Max has had enough and shoots P.J. in the hand)

Max: *I'm not having it P.J. If you want to die slow then that's up to you!*

P.J.:   *Owww! What the f'*#@! Now what was that all about I didn't say I killed her I said you 'thought' I killed her. There's a big difference you know!*

Max: *Cut the crap P.J.!*

P.J.:   *I'm no good to you if I'm dead and it seems like you might have a missing persons case on your hands.*

Max: *Say what you gotta say P.J., I'm not intimidated by you.*

P.J.:   *Look Max, I know you're not one of the hard core Santiagos. You just happen to be in the same family. So give me some information on where I can find the persons responsible for murdering my family and I'm on my way.*

Max: *Are you nuts? That's my family we're talking about here! My brother, my uncles, my cousins they all lived a little dirty so that I could grow up with the option of being a clean cut coffee brat, sparing a few details of course! You want me to rat on them just so you can continue on your vigilante rampage? You're on a suicide mission P.J., suicide!!*

(Max's weapon is still cocked)

P.J.:   *(very angry then breaking down) I'm dead already do you hear me! I'm dead! There's NOTHING on the inside! I wasted a few stupid years of my life being a runner for your family. I sold myself out thinking that because I lacked any real education drug running was the only thing that I could do. I didn't want to hurt nobody and I didn't want nobody to hurt me! All I wanted to do was get out! Start a new business, run it honestly and continue on with my life but that's not what happened.*

Max: *(forces P.J. into a kneeling position and stands from behind) You don't f#*% with the Santiagos, got that P.J.?. You just don't do that! Ask anyone in the Delatorrez family. You haven't seen them lately lately have you? It's a shame how their warehouse just went up in flames isn't it? We Santiagos can take credit for that! And what about that little girl who came up missing in the LaSalle family, I believe her father was the police commissioner wasn't he? Poor thing, they never even found her. (beat) It's ugly business sometimes but my family's gotta maintain their respect. Y'know what I mean?*

P.J.:   *She's safe you know. Taylor's safe.*

Max: *But where is she?*

P.J.:   *You'll find that out when you put your gun down. (sensing Max's hesitancy) Go ahead put it down.*

Max: *(Places weapon within reach inside the waistband and belt clip but maintaining a sense of authority) This is some crazy sh*t!*

P.J.:   *(displays a photo) Take a look at this.*

Max: *This isn't Taylor?*

P.J.   *You're right. That's Pietro Juan Hernandez, a former suburban drug runner from Columbia. The Satiagos call him P.J.*

Max: *What?! P.J.?! What the F.... Where's my sister? (goes for the gun and points it to P.J.'s head)*

P.J. :   *Well I stopped in to see her early this morning and she's being detained by my associates.*

Max: *(cocking the gun) You've got two seconds to tell me who you are!!*

(the tension has reached a boiling point, the dialogue proceeds with rapid fire)

P.J.:   I'm Phoenix Johannsen.

Max: Phoenix Johannsen?

P.J.:   I'm a DEA Special Agent. They also call me P.J.
         Your P.J. was arrested last week.

Max: You got nothing on me so keep talkin' buddy!

P.J.:   Before you do anything rash, look out that window.

(Max looks out the window. Max's mind is racing)

P.J.:   *(continues) You're not yet under arrest yet but we did gather some information
         from your sister... and with you airing the family's dirty laundry like you just did
         we should finally have enough information to get some convictions on the Santiagos.
         As for anything else that happened here today, I'm sure my devices only kept track
         of the important stuff. And if you're wondering if that sharp shooter out there is any
         good (takes a quick glance towards the window), well one false move and it looks
         like we both die at the same time; that is of course if you are planning on pulling
         the trigger. It's your move Max, make a f*#`%ing decision!!*

Lights Out.

The End

What A Man's Gotta Do

A One Act

Characters: (ages open)
Karla   - sophisticated, no nonsense   Darwin -country, enthusiastic
Florence - a true diva, classy & fun   Paul   -down to earth, good natured
Lorene   - reserved, almost shy   Wesley -classy, well educated
Catreese - strong, demanding

Setting: a bare or versatile stage that can quickly suggest
       several settings i.e. an office, an auto shop, apartment and restaurant.

The next twenty four hours will hopefully produce a Valentine's Day
with three very romantic endings but whatever the case, a man's gotta do
What A Man's Gotta Do.

Scene 1:   The Randle Real Estate Agency

KARLA

(on the phone) Yes, that's right. The deal is final. Enjoy your new home.
Bye. (She hangs up and dials a new call.) Hello, yes this is Karla Furguson
and I'd like two dozen roses delivered to Nate's Garage downtown. The
card should read 'to Paul with love from your wife Karla, thanks for being
the love of my life.' Yes, oh yes the last four digits are 7272. Yep, that's it.
Thanks, bye bye. (hangs up.)

Lorene enters.

LORENE

Karla, the documents have been filed, the papers are drafted and the
calls have been returned.

KARLA

Thanks Lorene, I guess we're all done for today. Call Florence, maybe
we can all go out for a drink.

LORENE

Honey, Miss Florence finished early today. 'Said she had some shopping
to do for Wesley's Valentine's surprise.

KARLA

Well I'm spending the evening at home with Paul and I understand that
his friend Darwin is looking forward to meeting you. I hear he has a great
personality and he's very down to earth.

LORENE

Karla, if this date turns out to be a dud, I'm no longer working with you
and I'm never speaking to you again... (they chuckle).

KARLA

All right, all right, it's just that I don't want you to spend Valentine's Day
alone. C'mon, what have you got to loose?

LORENE

Now why do I feel like those words are gonna come back to haunt me?
Look, I'm outta here.

KARLA

Okay, have a good one.

Lorene exits.

KARLA

Now where is Florence. That woman has lost her mind since she met
that man. Let me just call that diva right now.

Florence bursts through the door loaded with shopping bags.

FLORENCE

(full of excitement) Boss Lady! Can you stand it? Am I the bargain queen or what? Look at this exquisite smoking jacket I got for Wesley! 'And what about this? It's the latest in men's fragrance and it's all the way from Italy. Oh and wait til you see this! (she pulls out an expensive piece of lingerie) Girl when I get through doing my own rendition of shake it fast, all Wesley will be able to do is say My, My, My and Danger, Danger, Danger!

KARLA

Whoa, slow down now. (jokingly) You know you don't get paid that much here and I think accounting told me that they lost your next paycheck.

FLORENCE

Oh I know I'm dizzy with love right now. I've waited so long to finally get a good man, I wanna make sure I treat him right.

KARLA

Well enjoy. I'm sure that Wesley will be blown away. I hope that he's everything that you've always dreamed of and more.
Now come on I'm starving. Where are we going for dinner?

end of Scene One.

Scene Two:
setting: Nate's Garage. There's an old radio in the background playing
        an uptempo James Brown song. Darwin and Paul are talking.
        Wesley enters later.

DARWIN

Paul Furguson, my main man! Thanks so much for hooking me
up with a beautiful black woman to spend Valentine's Day with!
Tell me 'bout her one mo' time!

PAUL

Darwin, Darwin, slow your roll or you're gonna blow it.
Her name is Lorene, she's attractive and she's worked with Karla
for about four years now. Where're y'all going tomorrow?

DARWIN

I'm having her meet me at Rubye's Soul Food Rotisserie down on
Denker Street. She said she like fine dining and I don't know no
finer cook than Rubye. She gon' be there cookin' herself tomorrow.

PAUL

'Hope you have a good time. Just try to play it cool okay.
Now as for me, man tomorrow night I'm gonna put a pair of
diamond earrings on Karla's ears and then I'm gonna give her an
envelope with tickets to the Bahamas in it!

DARWIN

Y'all goin' on a cruise....
PAUL

We're goin on a cruise man. The Furgusons are gonna sail the high
seas!

DARWIN

Man, that oughta be nice. I always did wanna see them Islands
and thangs like that.

A very well dressed man approaches. It is Wesley Johnson.

PAUL

Hey Wesley. Is your Jag giving you problems again?
(kidding) I told you those are some temperamental cars.

WESLEY

What's up Paul, Darwin. (to Paul) Naw man, everything is cool.
I was just checkin to see if the new rims came in yet. What y'all
up to?

DARWIN

Paul was just telling me how he was gonna make sure that he *gets*
some from his wife tomorrow night! (chuckles) And all he had to
do was save up for some diamond earrings. Y'know them married
guys can't be missing out on no holidays.

PAUL

(good natured about Darwin's cracks) Shut up man! See you talk
too damn much, that's why Lorene ain't gon' like your country ass.

DARWIN

(taking this one seriously) For real man?

PAUL

Naw fool, I'm just joking.

WESLEY

Wait a minute? Holiday, what holiday?

Paul and Darwin look at each other and then look at Wesley.

PAUL & DARWIN

Valentine's Day!!

WESLEY

Oh damn, Valentine's Day. Tomorrow? (beat) No wonder! Florence has been dropping all those hints about a *deeper commitment, family security* and *all that...* you know all that *stuff!* She's trying to tie a brother down! Shoot, I bet she's already got me measured for the tux!

PAUL

Well *is* she or is she *not* the ONE? Now I've known you for a long time Wesley and I think that she kinda sparks something in you that you still don't wanna deal with. Even players like you got a heart and I think Florence finally got to it.

WESLEY

(Trying to play it off, Wesley tries to make small talk with Darwin)
So what you doing tomorrow night man?

DARWIN

I'm taking Karla's friend Lorene out for fine dining and elegant conversation.

WESLEY

Yeah, with who?

DAWIN

That's cold man, (still good natured) don't let me have to whoop your Wall Street ass back to the south side where you came from.

WESLEY

Yeah well the only whooping that's going to be goin' on is me
whooping your sorry behind on the court tomorrow morning.
So where are you taking your date?

DARWIN

We're goin' to Rubye's Soul Food Rotisserie, they got a waitress now
and some tables, it's gon' be nice.

WESLEY

Rubye's down on Denker?

PAUL

(With an I told you so posture.) That's where he wanted to take her.

WESLEY

Ah that's grease and gravy man, nothin' but grease and gravy
buy hey y'all have a good time.

DARWIN

We gon' have a good time, when I get her back to my place I'm gon'
sop her up like a biscuit.

They all chuckle

WESLEY

All right I'm out.

PAUL & WESLEY

Okay 'bro stay up! 'Catch you later.

Wesley exits. Paul and Darwin murmur conversation while lights fade to black.

End of scene two.

Scene Three:
The next day back at the Randle Real Estate office. Karla and Lorene
are having casual conversation when Florence enters.

KARLA

So at about seven I 'm dropping the kids off at Grandma's so that
Paul and I can have the whole evening to ourselves.

LORENE

And what did Paul say when he got the flowers?

KARLA

He was a little embarrassed... y'know all the fellas teased him
but he loved them. He said he'd sprinkle the petals all over our
bed tonight.

LORENE

You mean to tell me it's still steamy like that!

KARLA

It still is steamy like that. Now we don't always agree on everything
but we've learned to fight without putting each other down. Sometimes
I gotta let him have it his way and sometimes I get to win a few but even
more than love, we have a deep respect for each other. Girl, he ain't
goin' nowhere and neither am I.

LORENE

So when are y'all posing for the *love* issue of Essence magazine?
(beat) It must really be nice. I wouldn't mind settling down again but
a lot of guys see my car and my house and they're either intimidated
or they want me to take care of them. 'And why do they all have bad
credit?

KARLA

(laughing) They don't all have bad credit? Do they? (shifting slightly)
I'll tell you what, we would be here until the same time next week
discussing the woes of male/female relationships. We've all made
mistakes and name one person that doesn't have a case of hindsight?
Just be smart, keep your heart open and keep your credit cards in
your purse.....

Florence enters blowing her fingernails.

FLORENCE

Hey ya'll! How you like this new fingernail polish... and do you see
my toes? Do *you* see my *toes?* Notice the capital "W" in rhinestones!

KARLA

Florence, girl sometimes you're just *one block* short of the ghetto
and you know I've known you long enough to say that.

FLORENCE

(warmly) Well you lived right down the block from me girlfriend.
Oh Karla. I'm just so excited that's all. I can't wait until tonight.

LORENE

Well I've got a date too tonight remember?

FLORENCE

That's right! Who're you going out with again?

Paul' friend Darwin.

FLORENCE

Darwin Winslow? Karla you set Lorene up with Darwin Winslow?
(as she's cracking up) I thought she was your friend.

KARLA

Florence, you'd just better hope you don't have to move in with
Lorene after you spend all your money on Wesley.

LORENE

(jokingly) She's not moving in with me. She's allergic to cats
and Muffy's not going anywhere.

FLORENCE

You all had better leave me alone before I make you wear lime
green polyester for your brides maids dresses and Karla you know
green is not your color.

KARLA

Yeah and polyester makes me itch.

LORENE

So what does Mr. Wesley have planned for you Florence?

FLORENCE

I don't know. He's been kinda quiet, almost a little distant.
(starting to think very seriously, then she snaps out of it) But hey,
It's all good. We're gonna have a ball! (to Lorene) So is Darwin
taking you to meet his mama, (to Karla) you know he lives with
his mama don't you?

KARLA

Florence, he does not still live with his mama. She died. The house
is all his now but he does still have all those broke down cars in the back.

LORENE

Oh my God, see that's why I hate blind dates. Does Darwin have dogs?

KARLA

No, the dogs died too but he does have some fish.

LORENE

Gold fish? I like gold fish.

KARLA

No catfish, he's got a pet catfish.

FLORENCE

Don't listen to me Lorene, this guy could be your Prince Charming.
He could, what in the world do I know about it? If I knew so much
I'd be happily married like Karla.

Silence. Lights fade.

End of Scene Three.

Scene Four.

Wesley's house where he sits in front of a TV set with the game on.
He is casually dressed and airing out his thoughts.

WESLEY

(thinking out loud) Man, Florence is one special lady.... naw, she's just
another honey... man NAW, NAW MAN, naw HELL NAW (Wesley is
really trying to convince himself that he hasn't completely fallen for
Florence)! She's just a fly ass woman, with an incredible mind...
she's funny.... she understands me... she gives me my space... she's got
a deep spiritual side... she makes nice money.... so she won't try to
take my money... and she loves me. She loves me for me. (to himself)
Hey fool she loves you! And she's got that Taa Dow!! (indicating
Florence's well endowed physique) Florence is all that but I don't need
to be settling with just one woman? Do I? I mean, I'm educated, I look
good, I make good money, I haven't been incarcerated, I don't drink,
I don't do drugs, I'm straight. Hey I'm a commodity! I can't take myself
off the market like that. What if we hook up and she goes crazy? What if
she gains weight? What about the kids? (beat) Shoot I don't want no damn
kids... yes I do... NO, I don't.... yeah, I guess a couple of hard heads running
around would be all right... 'knowing Florence, she's probably wanna adopt
the whole neighborhood. Yeah, maybe we can just adopt a kid and
then she won't loose her shape like my mama did. My youngest brother is
twenty four and she's still blaming her size on us. (still thinking) Wesley,
Wesley hold up a second.... I think I love this girl. Wait, did I say the "L"
word? (with this realization Wesley has a baby temper tantrum like a child
whose mother has just taken his lollipop) I haven't been in love since my
college girlfriend left me for a ball player. I swore I'd never trust another
woman again. Damn, I think I'm in love with Florence, this can't happen
to a player like me, a brother's supposed to be harder than that! Whew,
I think I better take a shower.

End of Scene Four.

Scene Five:

Paul and Karla's house Valentine's night. Karla is wearing the earrings and
she holds the cruise tickets in her hand. Romantic music plays in the background.

KARLA

Paul, we've been married ten years and you're kissing my fingertips
like it's our honeymoon.

PAUL

What honeymoon? Baby you know I couldn't afford to take you on
a honeymoon but you loved me still. You hung in there with me during
the lean times and you never made me feel like I was less than a man,
even when we disagreed.

KARLA

Paul, you never gave me a reason to do anything but love you. Yeah,
we had misunderstandings but you never, ever treated me with disrespect.
You never called me out of my name, you never spoke ill of my career
and you supported me too my dear. Sometimes all I needed was a strong
arm to hold onto and a big bear hug at the end of the day and no matter
what you were going through, you gave me that, you gave me that honey.

PAUL

Well baby girl, it's like this. I may have had a chip on my shoulder at
times but I tried not to take that out on you. This ain't a world that
honors a man for having a little grease under his fingernails and sometimes
I'm not proud of the fact that I didn't have more to offer you and the kids.
A lot of time I was just angry at myself. I wanted so much more for
myself, so much more and then I look at you and I think, man what
did I do to deserve this woman? You're beautiful, you're successful
and you're....

KARLA

...and I'm yours.

PAUL

Can you believe that? We made it Karla, we made it ten years.

KARLA

We made it because we're a team Paul. Who knows what may have
happened to me if you hadn't come along. I'm sure I would have
worked hard and done all right in life but I might have been somewhere
in a big condo with a closet full of designer labels but with no man
and no child and trying hard to find new ways to make me happy.

PAUL

You accepted me Karla. You accepted my blue collar, you accepted
the fact that I had a child, you accepted my bad credit and all of my
mistakes. You gave me a reason to want to do right.... 'he that findeth
a wife, findeth a good thing.

KARLA

Oh Paul, do your friends know that you know how to break it down
to a woman like this?

PAUL

When you weren't looking, I read your old magazines.

KARLA

Thank you for a wonderful Valentine's Day...

PAUL

No honey, thank you.

They embrace. Lights fade out on them and up on Lorene who is in a restaurant
waiting for Darwin who rushes in. A gritty blues song plays in the background.

DARWIN

Sorry I'm late sugar, my car broke down... 'damn Buick!
But it's all taken care of. I told the waitress to sit you right here
next to the window so I'd know which one you was!

LORENE

Hi Darwin. 'Nice to meet you. I must say that's a nice *black*
suit you're wearing... and those *brown* shoes are pretty fancy too
but not as spiffy as that *blue* tie.

DARWIN

Why thank you. Listen darlin' order anything you want on the menu.
You know this first date is on me and the sky's the limit.. but I
recommend the ox tails!

Lights out. The end of Scene Five.

Scene Six:

Wesley's house. He is hurriedly getting dressed for an evening out. As he's splashing
on his after shave and buttoning his shirt when the phone rings. He lets his answering
service pick up.

WESLEY

(answering machine message) Hi, this is Wesley I'm not in at the
moment but leave me a message and I'll get back to you as soon
as I can. (beep sfx)

CATREESA (voice over only)

(On the answering machine.) Wesley, this is Catreesa, call me
immediately! It's urgent. (beep sfx)

WESLEY

Ah man, (checks is watch) I'm running late as it is. (he's briefly perplexed
then he decides to make a call)   Hi Florence.... yeah, everything's okay but
hey , can you meet me over here, I don't wanna miss our reservation and
I'm going to need just a couple more minutes.   Okay, see you when I you
here.

Wesley's cell phone rings.

WESLEY

(He grabs it on the first ring) Yeah, what's up? (he was not expecting
the person on the line) Catreesa, hey ah, I just got your message I was
gonna.... WHAT, you're at my door?

He goes to the door with cell phone in hand. He opens it and we see a very upset Catreesa in the door way also with a cell phone in hand.

CATREESA

(As she fold up her phone.) Hi Wesley, I'm sorry for just barging over here like this, I was on the cell phone when I called you the first time. Honey, I need you so much right now. (she breaks down in tears)

WESLEY

Ah, 'Treesey what's wrong, I mean what's up, I'm about to step out and...

CATREESA

Wesley, sit down...

WESLEY

I don't want to sit down, just tell me what it is baby... I got an appointment to get to.

CATREESA

That's right I know you said you were working tonight.
(It's awkward but she's gotta come out with it) Wesley, I'm pregnant...

WESLEY

You're what?

CATREESA

I mean, *we're* pregnant, I guess that's what I should say.

Just then we hear the door bell ring right on cue.

WESLEY

Ah man, that's my boy! Look let me get rid of him.

Door bell rings again.

WESLEY

Ah, in a minute!

CATREESA

If that's your boy, I'd like to meet him, just not right now. We really need to talk baby.

FLORENCE

(from outside) Wesley, honey where are you?

Catreesa hears the woman's voice and darts to the door. She whips it open.

CATREESA

This ain't *your boy* Wesley and it doesn't look like she's dressed for no business meeting.

We see Florence who is simply stunning in a red dress, she also has a few packages that are all intended for Wesley.

FLORENCE

(both hurt and confused) Wesley, what's going on?

WESLEY

Ah Catreesa, why don't *you* wait for me in the other room while I speak to *this* young lady for a moment.

FLORENCE

(in disbelief but not nasty at this point) "Young Lady?" Since when did I become some "young lady" to you Wesley?

CATREESA

(completely petered now) I ain't going no damn where! I came here to discuss something with you Wesley and that's what I'm gonna do.

WESLEY

(still trying to maintain control over the situation) Ah, Florence why don't we step outside then....

FLORENCE

(obviously hurt) I'm not going anywhere until you tell me what's going on?

CATREESA

Tell her Wesley! Tell her we've been together for the past two years now...

WESLEY

Catreesa, will you shut up! This is my house! Not yours!!!

FLORENCE

Tell me what Wesley, tell me what? Is this your wife? Have you been married this whole time?

CATREESA

No, I'm not his wife but I am carrying his baby and if he ever wants to see his child then he'd better settle things with you because I'm not going anywhere!

FLORENCE

Wesley, is this true?   *Can* this be true?

WESLEY

Ah.... well... ah...

This is a difficult moment as each character tries to cover their hurt
and shame.

FLORENCE

(not even looking at Catreesa but staring directly at Wesley)
Happy Valentine's Day Wesley (she slowly lays down each
package for him, gathers her dignity)   I loved you completely
and honestly.

Florence exits.

End of Scene Six.

Scene Seven:

We see the Furguson house where Karla, Lorene and Florence have convened.

FLORENCE

How could I have been so stupid? I knew he was too good to be true.

KARLA

It's not stupid to love someone with all your heart but it is stupid for
a man to have unprotected sex! 'And to lie about his activities well that's
a weak man as far as I'm concerned. You told me that he said he was
seeing you exclusively. I don't care how many suits he's got or how
much money he makes, he ain't no man to me. He put both your lives
in danger!

Florence tries to hold back her tears but can't.

KARLA

I gotta tell ya' I thought Wesley was The One as well but thank God you found out what he was really made of.

LORENE

It may sound old fashioned but I'm going the plain old, straight laced biblical route my next time around. I don't care how long it takes me I want to know under what grounds and to what lengths a man has master self control... and you know what part of his 'self' needs to be controlled.

FLORENCE

I just don't understand, I never wanted anything but love and honesty. Sometimes black women get such a bad rap when it comes to supporting our men, trusting our men, respecting them and caring for them. I didn't give a damn about Wesley's pay check. I mean it was nice that he had one but I've worked hard to have my own paycheck. I worked hard to go to school. Is it wrong to want a man of equal status? Should I automatically assume that every man in a nice suit with a nice job is a dog.

KARLA

Florence, it doesn't matter what the man does for a living, of course you want someone with some level of intelligence but a man has got to be ready! He not only has to have enough of shuffling his women, he's got to have enough of himself... lying and covering up and explaining himself out of all kinds of situations. Honey before Paul and I got together he admits that he was a real dog!

FLORENCE

Paul?

KARLA

Yes Paul! As a result he has a child from an angry woman who has vowed that he'll never see his child again. The child's mother could not come to terms with the fact that Paul never loved her. So she tried to manipulate Paul with the child, when that didn't work, she moved out of the country. That's something that Paul and I both have to live with. He's a great father to our children but you always miss the one that got away.

LORENE

I don't respect women who use children in that way. That child is still going to want to know his father. He's gonna think his daddy just doesn't care.

KARLA

Yeah, then there's the father's who really don't care.

LORENE

You mean like mine?

FLORENCE

My father was always there for us. He cared for my mother, he was faithful to her and to us and I never saw them have a cross word. I just wanted to the same thing for myself.

LORENE

Sometimes the only happy endings are the ones we create for ourselves. I'm through chasing love and I'm through being a prisoner to love. No more blue weekends, no more blind dates, I'm going to get busy and discover a purpose for my life other than wishing for a man. And Karla, tell Paul that Darwin is the countriest man I have ever met in my life. Yes I do like him, but only as a friend.

FLORENCE

My feelings are swinging like a pendulum right now, I don't know
if I'm more hurt or angry. I don't know if I love him or hate him at
this moment. Should I even listen to anything he has to say?

KARLA

What can he say? I think he told you a lot about the trust factor and
that's the backbone of any relationship. Y'know I used to be an angry
bitter person. 'Seems like I was always just a heartbreak away from
cussing somebody out... that is until I got a life threatening disease.
I either had to chill out or die. I thought about, my husband, my
children and all the things I looked forward to. I had to pray a lot,
I went to counseling, I read a lot of books and I had to forgive
EVERYBODY! I found a new light, a new love and a new piece
inside of me. I found a new sense of control and freedom. If it weren't
for that I may not have seen past Paul's pick up truck
and dirty fingernails. I saw his soul because I had cleansed my soul.

FLORENCE

I think, I'm just gon' go solo for a while. I'm temporarily retiring
from the game.

LORENE

Don't rush things Florence, if you like ox tails and calf liver, Darwin
just might be your guy.

They manage a loving chuckle as Lorene and Karla give Florence a loving
embrace.

End of Scene Seven.

Scene Eight:

Nate's Garage

Paul and Darwin are talking. Wesley enters later.

DARWIN

I'm too nice that's what it is! They never like the nice guys.

PAUL

I don't think that's what it is. It's just that some people
connect and some people don't.

DARWIN

I think she does like me a little bit though, she just don't know it yet.
See, I got everything a woman needs. I got property, automobiles,
I got a good head on my shoulders....

PAUL

I know buddy, you're the man. Don't even sweat it. You'll find the
right one.

Wesley enters. He looks like he's been up all night.

WESLEY

I blew it! I think I finally found the right girl and I blew it!

PAUL

Hey what happened Wesley, what's bugging you man?

WESLEY

(long beat) I don't even know how to explain... I, I... um.
I had been spending a lot of time with Florence.... a *lot* of time
with her. I mean, we were chillin' like I've never kicked it with
a chick before. I mean, it was *on*, man it was *ON!* But ah... I, ah...

DARWIN

Wesley what happened man, you're scaring me...

WESLEY

I just couldn't let it go... I just had to hit it one more time.

PAUL

Hey, Bro' you're not making sense. Are you okay? Is it some kind
of disease? What is it?

WESLEY

Yeah, it's a disease! It's when you can't turn down another piece of booty!
And now she's pregnant!

PAUL

Florence is pregnant?!

WESLEY

No Catreesa is pregnant.

PAUL & DARWIN

Catreesa?!

WESLEY

Yeah Catreesa. She was my old lady for a while, well not really my
old lady but we were 'associates'... y'know friends... or whatever you
want to call it. I was never really that serious about her, it was something
to do that's all... and I had a few other friends as well.

DARWIN

Ah man, women don't look at that stuff like we do man. Most of the time
it ain't no game to them, they'll get serious on you. Even I know that.

PAUL

Wesley, listen to me. Get your head together man. Now what do you
want to do?

WESLEY

I don't know what I want to do.

PAUL

I know it's hard but just figure it out man, I don't want to see you
do the same foolish thing that I did. Many a babies have been made
from just casually screwing around. It was a screw to you, it meant
much more to her and then she sets out to punish you and the child
because you don't want to be one big happy family.

WESLEY

I was gonna break it off with her man, I just had to have her one more
time. (beat) I didn't want to have no kids with her, *not her*. I mean
she's all right but that's not who I could see myself coming home
to every day.

DARWIN

I know that's right. If it's the Catreesa I think it is, that woman is
crazy, she'll have all your business on the Jerry Springer show if
you're not careful.

Think of the child, Wesley. How do you see yourself in the life
of this child, that's what's most important. By the time I figured out
what I wanted to do, my child's mother was so angry at me for not
being around *and* for marrying someone else that she moved out
of the country and there wasn't a thing I could do about it. I had
no legal documents on the child and I had no record of child support.
The blessing for me was that Karla came along after most of
that drama was behind me. I wouldn't want to be in your shoes
right now.

WESLEY

(with regret) I thought I was so invincible. I was so smooth with
all my situations now I've got a child who's gonna need me, a woman
who loves me and another woman who's gonna take me for all I've got.

PAUL

Wesley, a man's gotta do, what a man's gotta do. Be financially responsible,
spend time with your kid but also know your legal rights. At this point I
suggest you find out what's really going on inside of you! You do have
choices but remember it's one thing to make a baby, it's another thing
to build a family. What kind of family are you going to build and with
whom? Now come on man, Miss Ruybe is having a two for one special
today ain't that right Darwin.

DARWIN

That's right, the special today is chicken feet and brown rice and
you have no idea how a good plate of food can change your mood.
Why you think I'm so happy all the time.

WESLEY

Ah no, not the grease and gravy express? Hey look, my car is a two
seater.

PAUL

That's all right man, we can all ride in Darwin's old Buick.

DARWIN

We sho' can, I just gotta rush out and move a few of my papers off the
front seat.

As Paul comforts Wesley, Darwin rushes out first, followed by the rest.
They ad-lib about Darwin's old truck or some of the menu items at Rubye's
Soul Food Rotisserie.

The End.

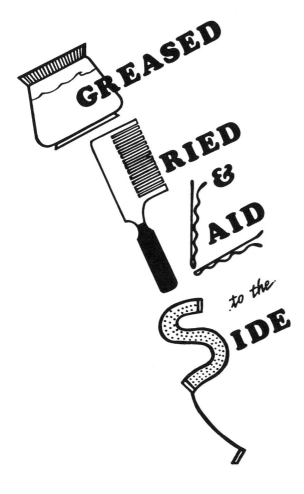

By LaRita Shelby

Copyright c. 1989

From the playwright...

This play is dedicated to all those who have touched and inspired my life. Even those who have caused me the deepest pain and disappointment have made their contributions unknowingly. I thank God the Father for guiding my hands across these pages. I hope that the seed falls upon good ground.

To mom, dad, Aunt Mary and Uncle Bill, Elvin and Dr. Mayme Clayton,

With Love,

LaRita!

The time:	Sometime in the present.
The setting:	Los Angeles, California
The place:	The Glamour Gallery, the place where hair magic is performed and hopefully beauty is achieved. Today like any other Saturday, The Gallery is filled with the salon regulars and a few first time patrons who have come to have their services performed. A few fireworks are definitely on the horizon when the self centered and the self righteous attempt to mix and all too boldly point out the faults in *each other* with little or no regard for the faults in themselves. For many of these people, their hair style represents a status symbol and often reflects their reversed sense of values. When the reflection is turned from their highly groomed and obviously *together* exteriors will they be as eager to admit that their interiors are in dire need of a *touch up*. The audience needs only to see that this is the waiting area of the salon. The receptionist should have a telephone with an intercom system on her desk. The salon may be decorated with appropriate posters, and an end table with magazines on it.

The Characters

Receptionist: (age open) She can be cordial but she'll get an attitude in a minute. She is just there doing her job and doesn't display any particular concern for anybody but herself. She's not nasty but she's also not the most personable person in the world. She has no real goals for herself. Through out the show she is on the phone in communication with the hair technicians who the audience never sees.

Cleola Frazier: (a.k.a. Ms. Got the Scoop, age open) She will be friendly to anyone just so that she can get into their business. She knows about what everybody else is doing. She's got the dirt on *everyone*. She's so busy keeping up with everybody else's business, she hasn't even noticed her life is a royal mess.

Sis. Petunia Patterson:
(Ms. Busy Body) A genuine sweet lady who is so far gone in keeping up with the Jones' that she has forgotten which Jones' she's keeping up with. She's the best dressed at her church because her minister told her so. She simply has to have everything matching or she can't leave the house. She's been so busy buying things that she's overlooked the fact that she's totally over extended financially and that she owes her first born to creditors at high interest rates. She's not concerned about saving or investments. Her biggest investment is in her closet and her hat collection... after all she is the *best dressed* woman at church because her minister told her so. Sister Patterson is also over loaded with packages and she runs in and out of the mall during the play to buy more things.

Ms. Gretta Gucci: Young, sassy and sophisticated to the maximum is Gretta Faye Gucci. She simply has to have designer *everything!* She has been courted and escorted by everyone who is anyone. According to her, there is something physically wrong with everyone. Either their nose is too large, their eyes are too close together or something else is wrong with them. She is always coifed. Oh and by the way, she would literally be devastated if anything ever happened to her physical beauty or her material possessions since that's all she has going for her.

Afrika Akeem Abdul: He only stops by the salon to have his 1970's afro re-shaped. He is draped with Peace signs and symbols of Africa. He blames the white man for the fact that he hasn't had a good job in ten years. He dropped out of the white man's school, the white man's religion and the white man's work force. In his view, everyone else in the world is grossly misled and he is the only sane warrior left. Afrika has also resolved that black women are all screwed up.

Mrs. Phelps:	She is a loving mother of her teenage daughter Muriel. Mrs. Phelps is almost wimpish to the requests of her daughter. She is nurturing to a fault. She buys her daughter everything she wants. She does everything for her daughter and she's convinced that because she is doing this, her daughter is certain to make good in life. It's been ages since she sat down to study with her daughter or review her homework or went to church with her. The thought of talking to Muriel about sex, disease or birth control or drugs is out of the question. Mrs. Phelps lives through her daughter. She only comes to the salon to get her daughter's hair done. She wears a wig.
Muriel Phelps:	Sweet sixteen and adorable. She is simply her mother's trophy piece.
Mr. L. L. Cool Jones:	He comes to the salon to get his J'heri curl (fade or corn rows) revitalized. He his draped in gold and the finest of designer athletic gear. He is a homeboy from the hood and he flashes lots of cash that he has retrieved from questionable sources. For him, it's all about making some fast cash, period!
Mr. Ramon Reeves:	(Mr. GQ - Mr. Look So Good) He probably has a chain of women a mile long but that's okay because he has a certain understanding with all of them. He thinks that women expect too much anyway. He has good looks, impeccable style so a new woman is always just a smile away. He is a career man who visits the salon his monthly texturizer and manicure.
Ms. Diva Dunlap:	(late 20's to mid 30's) Ms. Diva is disillusioned to say the least. Though it may not be apparent at first, she is flustered and suffering an identity crises. She's had her share of disappointments and some marginal success. At the moment, all she can see is what' wrong with her and all that she counts are her failures. She's at the shop to get a hair weave. She is convinced that this new look will give her the boost that she needs. She has scraped up enough money to have this transformation performed.
Mayme Cantrell:	(Mid 30's or older) Mayme has a casual, down to earth quality about her. She is confident and doesn't need to impress anyone. She is not concerned with everyone else's business. She comes to the salon to get a press and curl. Mayme is striving to be the best that she can be. She loves God, she loves her fellow man and she loves herself with or without cosmetic enhancement.

Act One:

We see a lobby area of a moderately stylish beauty salon complete with about ten to twelve chairs, a magazine table and a reception desk. Presently we see no one seated in the waiting area. The receptionist is seated at her desk and she's talking on the phone.

Receptionist

Ohh yes girl, she came in here looking *tore up*. She looked a God awful mess, talk about naaappiiee.... What?! Yes I *know* this is the beauty shop but she didn't have to look *that* bad, she'll scare away some of our regular clients... You know the kind who get their hair done *every* week. Ha ha ha... oooh girl, yes you know we went up on our prices.... Why? ...because the son of a guns don't tip that's why! 'Gotta make it somehow... and we still got them old ladies coming in for a blue rinse... ah huh... yea.

CLEOLA ENTERS.

Receptionist

Ooooh child, I got to go, my customer is coming. Okay bye. (to customer) Hello, may I help you?

Cleola Frazier

Good morning, I'm Cleola Frazier. (with speculation) You're new aren't you? Well at least new to me. Honey, that last receptionist was a doozy! She was lazy, she was slouchy and she has a sour attitude...

Receptionist

She is my sister and she doesn't work here anymore.

Cleola

(quick change of attitude, from surprised to sorrowful) Oh, she doesn't? What a shame you can't keep good help these days... did you say that sweet child was your sister?

Receptionist

That's okay, she works my nerves sometimes too but I love her. (noticing her hair) I see you haven't been in for a while. What are you having done today?

Cleola

I have a nine o'clock appointment with Tyrone and I'm getting a touch up, a deep conditioner, a trim and I want my hair crimped.

Receptionist

Okay, Ms. Frazier. Have a seat. Tyrone will be with you shortly. He's working on a client.

Cleola

Working on a client?

Receptionist

Yes. That's right.

Cleola

But it's nine o'clock in the morning! When did the boy get here, six o'clock?

Receptionist

Six thirty. Now please have a seat.

Cleola

(reluctantly takes a seat as she mumbles to herself) Every time I come here, no matter what time, I've got to wait around to get my hair done. I just get so bored sitting here with nothing to do.

SHE PICKS UP A MAGAZINE AND BEGINS TO FLIP THROUGH IT. MEANWHILE SISTER PETUNIA PATTERSON ENTERS DRESSED TO KILL WITH MATCHING SUIT, HOSIERY, PURSE AND GLOVES. SHE HAS THAT "MARY KAY" "BARBARA WALDEN" LOOK ABOUT HER. SHE'S LOADED WITH PACKAGES.

Receptionist

Hi, who are you here to see?

Sis. Patterson

Hello, my name is Sis. Petunia Patterson and I'm here to see Miss Florence.

Receptionist

What are you having done?

CLEOLA LOOKS UP FROM HER MAGAZINE TO INSPECT WHAT'S
GOING ON.

Sis. Patterson

Oh, a shampoo and set as usual and... (whispering) I guess I'll have her touch up
my gray. It's Women's Day at church tomorrow, you know.

Receptionist

Okay, have a seat over there. It should only be a few minutes.

SIS. PATTERSON SITS AND PICKS UP A MAGAZINE. BOTH SHE AND CLEOLA
HAVE MAGAZINES BUT CLEOLA KEEPS LOOKING UP FROM HERS TO STARE AT
SIS. PATTERSON. SIS. PATTERSON DOESN'T NOTICE AT FIRST BUT THEN SHE'S SURE
SOMEONE IS WATCHING HER. SHE LOOKS UP AND CATCHES CLEOLA IN HER STARE.

Cleola

Excuse me, don't you go to First Baptist?

Sis. Patterson

(slow to be friendly at first) ...Yes.

Cleola

Didn't you speak for the Women's Day program one year?

Sis. Patterson

...Yes.

Cleola

Sister Petunia Patterson!

Sis. Patterson

That's right.

Cleola

(going on and on) I thought it was you when you walked in the door but I wasn't too sure. Now I saw that you were dressed sort of nice and I remembered that you *did* use to always dress sort of nice. Honey how is your husband?

Sis. Patterson

(mood still unchanged) ...and you are?

Cleola

Cleola Frazier. My ex-husband fixed your brother in law's car and invited us to church one time to hear you speak.

Sis. Patterson

(finally recognizing her) Ooh, Cleola. How have you been?

Cleola

Oh pretty good, Sis. Patterson. Except for this place. Every time I come in here I have to sit around all day before I get my hair done. 'And did you get a load of that *new* receptionist? She claims that she's the sister of the *old* receptionist. How you like her?

Sis. Patterson

She's all right I guess...

Cleola

(cutting her off since she didn't take the bait to talk about the receptionist) You sure do look nice Sis. Patterson. Where do you buy your clothes?

Sis. Patterson

(on this, she comes alive) Oh thank you? Well this suit in particular, I had made by one of the deacon's wives at church. I bought the panty hose at Penny's, I got the shoes at Kennys and I bought the hat at Jenny's and my sister gave me the earrings and purse. Now I like Leoman's but sometimes their things are picked over so that's why I also like to browse in Roberts and May but sometimes their clothes look so cheap... I usually buy my matching slips, girdles and brassieres there. But honey, if you really want to find some fine things you take yourself to Rodeo (ro-day-oh) Drive. They had a pair of $450.00 shoes there that I just had to have!

Cleola

You bought a pair of shoes for $450.00?

Sis Patterson

'Had to. They matched my Patrick Kelly gown to a tee. I had to look good for the Pastor's anniversary.

Cleola

How can you afford that?

Sis. Patterson

I can't. Well not all at once. That's why I charged them. Girl, a good charge card is the closest thing to God.

Cleola

Every time I see you Sis. Patterson you *sure are sharp.*

Sis. Patterson

'Got to. Honey I go to one of the largest churches in this city. If one of my members sees me *not* dressed, my reputation is ruined.

Cleola

What do you mean?

CLEOLA SITS IN CLOSE EXPECTING A JUICY RESPONSE.

Sis. Patterson

My pastor made me stand up in church one Sunday and he proclaimed that I was the best dressed woman in his congregation, next to his wife of course. He said that. He sure did, right after he preached that sermon about them dry bones in the valley. Girl, I was so elated I went out that same Sunday and bought two outfits just because.

THEY CHUCKLE. SIS. PATTERSON PULLS OUT A STRING OF ABOUT FIFTEEN PICTURES FROM HER WALLET. ON THE OTHER SIDE OF EACH PICTURE IS, WHAT ELSE, A CREDIT CARD. CLEOLA HAS SENSED THAT PETUNIA IS NO POTENTIAL GOSSIP PARTNER SO SHE'S RETURNED TO HER MAGAZINE.

Sis Patterson

Excuse me Cleola. Since you did happen to ask me about my clothes, I just happen to have photos of a few of my favorite outfits.

Cleola

(looking at the photos in disbelief) You have a hat to go with every outfit?

Sis. Patterson

That's right. This is from the ground breaking of the new Baldwin Jungle Mall. I'm wearing a brick red gabardine and silk ensemble with a pillbox hat and matching construction boots. Now this one is from the annual church picnic... I call this outfit Lilies Of The Fields because of the floral print on my hat, blouse, pants and shoes. Oh yes, yes... this is one I can't forget. I wore this outfit to the Ebony Women's Forum. It's an annual hoopla. You know snobs on the outside, snobs on the inside. I wanted to fit in so I wore all black. And I had this outfit ordered from China to match my new car. Speaking of China... excuse me.

SHE GETS UP AND GOES TO THE RECEPTION DESK.

Sis Patterson

(to the receptionist) Is Mai Ling Woo here today? I want to get my nails done too.

Receptionist

Yes she is. I'll put you down.

Sis. Patterson

Thank you. (she crosses back to Cleola) Watch these packages for me. I'm gonna make a mad dash through the mall while I'm waiting.

Cleola

No problem at all. Take your time. You just take your time.

SIS. PATTERSON EXITS AS MS. GRETA GUCCI CASCADES INTO THE ROOM.

Greta

(to receptionist) Excuse me, I'm Greta Faye Gucci and I'm here for my appointment with Pierre, King of Hair.

Receptionist

Oh yes, of course. Please take a seat.

AS GRETA SACHETS ACROSS THE FLOOR CLEOLA BLATANTLY STARES HER UP AND DOWN. GRETA SITS AND PICKS UP A MAGAZINE. SHE FLIPS THROUGH IT UNTIL SHE SPOTS SOMETHING VERY DISTASTEFUL.

Greta

(to Cleola) Excuse me but can you believe that she would wear *those* shoes with *that* dress in *this* magazine? Oh I'm embarrassed for her.

Cleola

Oh yes girl. It's a pure shame to be seen like that.

Greta

(she flips to another page) And look at this! This is just plain tacky. Tacky, tacky, tacky.

Cleola

Ah ha, sure is.

Greta

Now, look at her hair. She should've stayed at home.

Cleola

(baiting her) Huh hum, you're right about that one too. That reminds me of some of those tacky folks you see shopping out there in that mall.

Greta

(quite cocky) I don't shop in the mall.

Cleola

(obviously lying) Neither do I.

Greta

I have to have all my clothes designer made. I just can't wear cheap clothes... they make me itch.

Cleola

You must be like that other big old woman who just left out of here. You must be a clothes-a-holic.

Greta

No, not really. I just don't like anyone else to have what I have. My own personal style and taste is so eloquent that I must make myself stand out. You see, I just can't *live* anywhere or *drive* any old car. I think I have royal blood in me.

Cleola

(under her breath) I think you got *Thunderbird* in you.

Greta

What's that?

Cleola

Ah nothin' child.

BEAT.

Cleola

(continuing) Just answer me something. Now I see women like you all the time and I wonder... Do you work, are you rich or just lucky? How is it that you afford a lifestyle like that?

Greta

Honey there are lots of ways. A while back I was dating this athlete and I knew just what to say to get my rent paid. And then there's this friend of mine that... well let's just say he's a businessman of sorts and he comes into a lot of money all the time and he helps me out. Then I have these other two partners who manage to come across stolen clothing, now mind you, they don't steal the clothes themselves... they just come across it, and they always cut me a good deal. I also know a few designers and occasionally I'll get pieces in exchange for modeling.

Cleola

So you're a model who accepts stolen property.

Greta

Ooh, no way. I'm a Christian. I didn't steal it. Stealing is wrong. Now as far as the model part, that's right.

Cleola

(a bit excited) Ooh, now that's interesting. How did you get into *modeling?*

Greta

Well when I was kid my folks never paid too much attention to me but I always had pretty clothes. So I would always play dress up and cut out pictures in fashion magazines.

Cleola

But I ain't never seen you in anything. Do you make any money?

Greta

I don't have to. When I look this good, I get taken care of. Men are always offering me presents just to be with them. I don't compensate my morals mind you. I just have a lot of friends. Actually, I would like to make a little more money.

Cleola

Why don't you open a school or teach? Or maybe you could do something else on the side.

Greta

Are you kidding? I can't afford classes and I can't be getting up all early in the mornings... I get bags under my eyes if I wake up too early, too many mornings in a row. (beat) What's your name?

Cleola

Cleola.

Greta

Cleola, I'm Greta. You look like a woman I can trust, not like the other snobs around here.

Cleola

I'm telling you the truth.

Greta

There are times when I would like to branch out a bit, you know, expand my horizons.
Sometimes I'd like to really learn something and see the world.

Cleola

Child, I used to talk foolish like that too when I was your age... used to sit up dreamin' all the time.
Huh, girl this world is a mess. It ain't gon' give you nothin.

Greta

But maybe...

Cleola

(cutting her off) You're a pretty child. I reckon you've seen more ceilings than Michael Angelo but you
better try to get one of them nice doctors or lawyers to marry you. Then you'll have a life. Don't let all
that beauty go to waste!

Greta

I guess you're right, as long as he's fine because between me and you, I can't be waking up to no ugly
man, especially if he's broke.

THEY LAUGH. JUST THEN BRO. AFRIKA AKEEM ABDUL ENTERS LOOKING LIKE A LOST
SOUL BROTHER FROM 1973, AFRO AND ALL. GRETA AND CLEOLA STOP FLAT IN THEIR
CONVERSATION TO CHECK HIM OUT.

Receptionist

Good morning, may I help you?

Afrika

As-Salaam-Alaikum! Sistah, I'm Brother Afrika Akeem Abdul. I am here for an appointment with Mr. Taylor.

Receptionist

(checking her book) ...Oh you mean Girard? I see it.

Afrika

No, I mean Mr. Taylor. You see sistah, that is what's wrong with the black woman. She's lost all respect for the black man.

THE RECEPTIONIST GIVES HIM A LOOK LIKE HE'S CRAZY.

Afrika

(continuing) She has forgotten her due place in society. She has severed her benevolence to Mother Africa while she strives to be a white washed, watered down, iconoclastic, ostentatious, female facade domiciled in an Ethno-European jungle.

Receptionist

And what makes you draw that conclusion?

Afrika

Look at all those chemicals you put in your hair. That's why you ain't got none sistah! 'And you're probably on those pills too.

Receptionist

Firs of all when I feel like I want to be influenced an inspired by a true African American warrior who's in touch with his roots and very much into the present I already have a date watching re-runs of Johnnie Cochran in the O.J. Simpson trial!

THE RECEPTIONIST CATCHES HERSELF LOSING HER TEMPER. SHE QUICKLY SNAPS
BACK TO HER FRONT DESK CORDIAL ATTITUDE.

                              Receptionist

(continuing) Now would you please have a seat until your name is called.

AFRIKA GATHERS HIS NEWSPAPER, APPLE HAT, AFRO RAKE AND HIS DIGNITY AND
PROUDLY STRUTS ACROSS THE ROOM TO HAVE A SEAT. CLEOLA AND GRETA LOOK AT
EACH OTHER IN DISBELIEF.

                                Cleola

(Whispers to Greta) Honey, did you hear that?

                                Greta

I sure did. No class, no class at all!

                                Cleola

Now, he just done gone plum crazy. Next his wife is gonna be wearing sheets and head rags and he's
gonna be selling bean pies on street corners in the name of Allah!

                                Greta

I never did understand brothers like that. He seems to have gone a bit over board.

SHE PICKS UP ANOTHER MAGAZINE AND THUMBS THROUGH IT AS SHE NOTICES A
VERY SEXY POP STAR WHO HAPPENS TO BE WHITE.

                                Greta

(continuing) Oh my God! Will you look at this man here.

CLEOLA LOOKS ON.

Greta

For him I'd wear a sign... 'If you don't see what you want, ASK!'

AFRIKA OVERHEARS THIS AND HAS TAKEN IN HER REACTION TO THE MAGAZINE. HE INTERJECTS.

Afrika

Sistah, I don't believe what I just heard! How can you sit there and lust over a white man?

Greta

(standing up to him) I don't care if he's green. If he's got some money and looks this good, consider it a done deal. I'm his!

Afrika

But sistah, after all the white man has done to us.   It's been two hundred years of bondage, oppression, segregation, degradation and discrimination and you my African violet would waste your precious petals on a milky way sugar daddy. Baby *I'm* your Mr. Goodbar!

Greta

You mean Mr. Good for nothing! First of all, you ain't got no job! You can't dress and as quiet as it's kept, you got B. O.

Afrika

B. O.?

Greta

Yes, baby. Body oder! I've seen you in the unemployment office quite a few times!

Afrika

And what were you doing there?

Greta

(obviously lying) I was dropping off my friend.

Afrika

Well for *your* information, I would rather collect unemployment *or* beg than to be demeaned by the white man's employment system. It is designed to keep the black man down by taking him away from his family for eight to ten hours a day so that his woman can fantasize over the handsome white doctors that play on those soap operas while her man is gone. While at work, the brother slaves and competes with other white men who really aren't superior but because they've had the advantage of better schools and because nepotism has allowed them the opportunity to advance, they *appear* to be superior. That's why I hate schools. They're for white people. They don't teach us the same thing they teach *them!*

JUST THEN WE NOTICE SIS. PATTERSON WHO RE-ENTERED TO HEAR ENOUGH OF THIS TO KNOW THAT THIS MAN NEEDS HELP. SIS. PATTERSON HAS A FEW MORE PACKAGES AND SHE STEPS INTO THE CONVERSATION.

Sis. Patterson

(to Afrika) Excuse me honey, now I don't mean to eavesdrop. I didn't hear all of what you said but I did hear enough to know that you need some help. Why don't you come to my church sometime and we can pray about some of these things that's got you confused.

Afrika

(almost angry) Don't you tell me about prayer. That's all part of the white man's religion. Every time you see a picture of God he's white! His son is white and all those dudes he hung out with were white, all white! They're all just gospel Klansmen. You see, if the white man can convince the Negroes that they're supposed to stay on their knees begging like dogs waiting for a pot of gold to burst through the clouds then he's got us right where he wants us-- doggie style.

UPON HEARING THIS SISTER PATTERSON SHAKES HER HEAD AS SHE TURNS TO CLEOLA.

Cleola

Child, he's so far gone he doesn't even know his clothes are out of style.

Receptionist

Ms. Greta Gucci, please come to the shampoo area.

GRETA EXITS.

Sis. Patterson

(to Cleola) Girl, you still here I see.

Cleola

Yep, I'm still here. I tell that Tyrone every time, I can't be waiting in no shop for five hours at a time and *every time* I sit here so long that I have butt corns.

THEY CHUCKLE

Sis. Patterson

Honey, you need to look in that new jewelry store they got in the mall out there.
I found some earrings that'll knock you out.

Cleola

I'll tell you what'll knock you out. Did you see that gal that just went in there?

Sis. Patterson

The one that African was talking to when I came in?

Cleola

That's the one. She's a little mixed up too honey. She got to have 'designer this' and 'designer that' and...

Sis. Patterson

Well you know clothes DO make the woman.

Cleola

Yes but the child ain't even got no job I don't think. Now, it ain't none of my business but I bet the clothes she's wearing right now is hot.

THEY CONTINUE TO MIMIC CONVERSATION AS RAMON REEVES ENTERS DRESSED TO KILL WITH A SOPHISTICATED STRIDE THAT REEKS CONFIDENCE. AS THE RECEPTIONIST LOOKS UP FROM HER DESK SHE IS VISIBLY THROWN BY THIS MAN'S DEMEANOR. HER MOUTH IS AGAPE.

Receptionist

May I help you?

Ramon

Yes princess, my name is Ramon.

Receptionist

And what would you like *done* to you?

Ramon

I'd like a texturizer and manicure from your next available operator.

                              Receptionist

Very well. Have you ever been here before? I don't see your card.

                              Ramon

Once, but that was a long time ago. My regular girl is out of town and so I thought
I'd give this place a try since I've seen so many *foxes* come out of here before.

BEAT

                              Ramon

(continuing) Did anyone ever tell you that you have a pretty smile?

                              Receptionist

(blushing) No.

                              Ramon

Well you do.

                              Receptionist

(blushing even more) Thank you!

                              Ramon

Would you like to go to dinner sometime?

                              Receptionist

...Perhaps.

Ramon

Well how about if I...

CLEOLA APPROACHES DESK INTERRUPTING RAMON'S ADVANCES.

Cleola

Excuse me! Does Tyrone know I'm here? I 've been sitting for 'bout an hour now and I don't have time for this. I'll go somewhere else. Every time I come here I have to put up with this mess...

RECEPTIONIST BECKONS RAMON TO SIT DOWN AS SHE CONTINUES TO ADDRESS CLEOLA.

Receptionist

Okay ma'am, I'll remind him that you're here. Would you like some coffee?

Cleola

No I don't want no damn coffee, this ain't Starbucks. I want to get my hair done!

Receptionist

Okay ma'am. Please sit down. I'll get someone for you as soon as possible.

RECEPTIONIST PICKS UP HER DESK PHONE AND MIMICS TALKING WHILE CLEOLA TURNS AWAY AND WALKS BACK TO HER SEAT.

Cleola

(muttering under her breath) Ain't nobody got all day to be sitting in no beauty shop.
I been coming to tis beauty shop too long for this...

SHE CROSSES BACK OVER TO THE SEATING AREA TO FIND THAT RAMON HAS TAKEN HER SEAT. THIS MAKES HER EVEN MORE PISSED.

Cleola

(continuing to Ramon) Pardon me Lover boy but I was sitting in that seat.

Sis. Patterson

(also liking the sight of Ramon) Oh Cleola.

Ramon

Oh, sorry sugar. Here ya go.

CLEOLA STARTS TO SIT DOWN IN A HUFF AS WE HEAR ON THE INTERCOM.

Receptionist V/O

Cleola Fraizer, please come to the shampoo area. Cleola Frazier.

CLEOLA COLLECTS HERSELF AND EXITS.

Ramon

(to Sis. Patterson) She's a little uptight I see.

Sis. Patterson

Oh she's just one of the nervous types. She'll be all right.

Receptionist

Mrs. Petunia Patterson. Your operator is ready to take you now.

SIS. PATTERSON GATHERS HER PACKAGES AND EXITS AS L.L. COOL JONES ENTERS.

Receptionist

Yes.

L.L.

Yo, like I called to see if my man Girad could hook me up with an appointment cause like tonight me and my homies got a meeting with some homies that are off the chain!

Receptionist

What is your name?

L.L.

L.L. *Cool* Jones.

Receptionist

Okay Mr. Jones what are you having done?

L.L.

Yo, like I need my curl (fade or cornrows) tightened up a bit. Tonight I need to be so fresh and so clean!

Receptionist

I don't see your name here Mr. Jones. What time did you call?

L.L.

Well actually I was *thinking* about calling but I didn't *actually* get around to it.

Receptionist

It figures. Sit down over there and I'll see if Girad can squeeze me in.

L.L.

You baby but can *you* squeeze *me* in sometime?

Receptionist

Mr. Jones, over there please!

L.L. STROLLS OVER TO THE SITTING AREA WHERE HE IS GIVEN STRANGE LOOKS BY BOTH AFRIKA AND RAMON.

L.L.

(giving Afrika an up and down look) Damn I know you did the 70's man but let it go man, let it go.

AFRIKA

I beg your pardon, Brother?

L.L.

Ah nothin' man, don't you dig his 'fro?

RAMON

Personally, "Brother" I think it's disgusting. *He* looks like a disappointment from the past and *you're* a disgrace to the future.

L.L.

Yo, homey? Now what did I do to you?

AFRIKA

(interrupting) No you two are the disgrace to African American manhood.
Look at you. (to L.L.) You got enough grease in your hair to deep fry a dolphin.
ALTERNATE LINE: (if the hair style of L.L. is other than a curl)
You up in here lookin' like Master Peon!

L.L.

(flashing a wad of money) Yo man, but I got B&B. Bucks and babes, BUCKS AND BABES!

Afrika

That's dirty money man and you know it.

L.L.

How I choose to make my living is my business. At least *I work* you know.

Afrika

Hey what's this? Everybody's dogging me out cause I don't walk around with some sissy manicure.
Can't a man still have some dirt under his fingernails and have dignity too?

Ramon

That's bullshit man, bullshit. Deep down inside you wish you could be a clean cut executive like me
but you lack the moral fiber to penetrate today's corporate structure.

L.L.

In other words, you don't want to work!

Afrika

Man, shut up. I sho' ain't taking no sh*t offa you!

Ramon

(very cool) Listen brothers. You can't smell like a rose when you're living like trash.

GRETA RE-ENTERS WITH A PLASTIC CAPE ON AND A PLASTIC CAP.
WE SEE HER EMBARRASSMENT AT FACING THE MEN LIKE THIS.

Receptionist

Ms. Gucci, have a seat right over there. Your conditioner has to stay on for a few minutes.

GRETA TRIES TO TIP TO THE DRYER WITHOUT BEING NOTICED BUT SHE IS SURPRISED
TO SEE RAMON.

Greta

(as her mouth drops) Ramon Reeves!

Ramon

Greta?

Greta

Yes, Greta.

RAMON HALF RISES FROM HIS SEAT TO GIVE HER A HALF HUG.

Greta

I knew the day would come when I'd see you again.

Ramon

How've you been?

Greta

I see your number changed...

Ramon

Well, ah....

Greta

And you moved too...

Ramon

I was meaning to call you.

Greta

You weren't meaning to do nothing. Let's face it, the only difference between you and a real dog is that you only walk on two legs.

Ramon

Hey Greta, I didn't deserve that. How did you make out from your little ah... operation, you know.

Greta

I made out fine, no thanks to you. It's nothing I haven't been through before.

Ramon

I'd really been thinking about you and I was going to call you but...

Greta

But what?

Ramon

Ah Greta, you know I'm a career man. I got things to do. I had to keep moving. You were getting too serious.

Greta

But Ramon, after all the time we spent together.

Ramon

It doesn't matter because we had an understanding from the beginning and if you went and developed feelings for me then that's *your* problem.

Greta

Ramon, I'm a human being not a robot. I can't be programmed.

Ramon

I don't care! You women run around all sucked in and painted up trying to trick some man into falling in love with you. Well, I've got more important things to think about. You women just... well you expect too much.

Greta

Expect too much?

Ramon

You want to be taken out. You want to be romanced and you always want to talk!
You want to about feelings and intimate things all the time.

.

Greta

And what's wrong with talking?

Ramon

Why do you always have to mix things up by talking? Why can't we just be together and fill each other's needs and leave it at that without getting all emotional.

Greta

If that's what you want then why don't you just pull up to a curbside and buy it, that way you get what you pay for. Why is it that you can keep company with a woman for months, eating her cooking, spending her time and sharing her body and all she ever is to you is a *friend*, just a *friend?*

Ramon

Look baby, it's my prerogative. I make sure that me and my lady friends have an understanding in the first place. After that, I really don't care I just keep moving. If one doesn't act right, another one will. There's enough pretty faces and hot bodies in this town to keep my social calendar well occupied.

GRETA FIGHTS BACK TEARS AND JUST STARES AT HIM IN DISBELIEF.
AFRIKA AND L.L. ARE LOOKING AT HIM WITH DISDAIN.

Receptionist

Greta Gucci, please report to the shampoo area.

GRETA EXITS.

Receptionist

Mr. Adbul, Girad will see you now.

AFRIKA STANDS AND SLOWLY EXITS INTO THE SALON AREA GIVING RAMON
A LONG LOOK OF DISGUST.

Afrika

(to Ramon, sarcastically) Smelling like a rose huh?

AFRIKA EXITS TO THE SALON AREA.

Receptionist

L.L. Could you please come to the desk.

L.L. APPROACHES DESK.

Receptionist

Your regular operator Girad is very backed up today so our new hair designer Phillip is here today and he's going to do you okay?

L.L.

Phillip? I don't know no Phillip?

Receptionist

Relax, we carefully screen all our designers before they're allowed to join our staff.

L.L.

He'd better be bad or I want my money back.

L.L. EXITS INTO THE SHAMPOO AREA. CLEOLA AND SIS. PATTERSON RE-ENTER THE WAITING AREA CHATTERING AWAY. ONE HAS HER HAIR BLOWN STRAIGHT AND THE OTHER HAS SOME HAIR CLIPS ON. THEY SIT AND CONTINUE TO CHIT CHAT AS MRS. PHELPS AND HER DAUGHTER MURIEL ENTER THE SALON AND APPROACH THE RECEPTION DESK.

Receptionist

Hi, may I help you?

Mrs. Phelps

Hi, I'm Mrs. Phelps and I'd like to know if there's someone here who can do my baby's hair. She has a piano recital tomorrow. (to Muriel) Don't you Muriel?

Muriel

Yes ma'am.

BEFORE MURIEL GETS A CHANCE TO ANSWER MRS. PHELPS CONTINUES.

Mrs. Phelps

She needs a touch up and her ends trimmed, but just a little bit. I can't have my child bald headed.

Receptionist

Well, we're booked kind of heavy right now but I may be able to work something out.
Will you be getting your hair done as well?

Mrs. Phelps

Ooh no, I haven't been to the beauty shop in years. This old wig will just have to do another Sunday but I want my baby to look pretty though.

Receptionist

All right. Please sit down over there and I'll get someone for you as soon as possible.
Ramon, they're ready for you in the back.

MRS. PHELPS AND MURIEL SIT AND RAMON EXITS.

Mrs. Phelps

Now Muriel, are you sure you mailed all those invitations to your recital because I would hate for any of my friends to miss it.

Muriel

Yes, Maam.

Mrs. Phelps

You can call your friends and tell them if any of my friends don't show up then they can come.

Muriel

Yes Maam.

Mrs. Phelps

Baby, you sure are going to look beautiful tomorrow. Do you like the yellow dress I picked out?

Muriel

Yes maam.

Mrs. Phelps

I thought you would. How about the white ruffle socks?

Muriel

Well...

Mrs. Phelps

Those are the cutest little kind I liked as a child but my mother never could afford, besides panty hose on teenagers is lewd.

Muriel

But mama...

Mrs. Phelps

I remember the day you took your first step. I knew then you were special. I vowed that I'd work my knuckles raw to make sure you had all the pretty things I never had... like your own room, a canopy bed, your own, PC, TV and VCR with cable and all... and not to mention piano lessons, karate lessons, French, Spanish and German lessons...

Muriel

Thanks mama but....

Mrs. Phelps

...and how you do all that and manage to be a good Student Council President, Girl Scout and church choir member I'll never know. And you never complain... (sweetly) Come to think about it you never say anything at all. That's why I don't mind riding the bus every day or working three jobs to make sure that my baby is happy. And for graduation you know I'm gonna get you a brand new car.

CLEOLA AND SIS. PATTERSON HAVE BEEN CATCHING BITS AND PIECES OF THIS CONVERSATION. THEY REACT.

Cleola

(to Sis. Patterson) If she's not careful that child may not live to see graduation.

Muriel

Mama, they're having Mother-Daughter day at school next week during Sex Education Week. Can you come with me on Monday?

Mrs. Phelps

Naw baby, I'll be at work. Besides there ain't a thing you need to know about no sex at this age. You just keep your mind on your studies. Only loose young ladies have their minds on such vulgar things. Anyway you've got a *long* time before that concerns you. Right now you don't need to know nothing!

Muriel

(she nobs, then continues) Mama I finished my genealogy paper. Do you think you'll have time to look it over with me before I turn it in?

Mrs. Phelps

Muriel, honey you know we'll probably be at the shop all day today and I work on Sundays. I'm lucky enough to get time off to come to your piano recital. That's why I want to make sure you look like Mama's little angel. Come to think of it, I'll be right back. Let me see if Stride Rite has some yellow shoes in your size.

SHE KISSES MURIEL ON THE FOREHEAD AND EXITS.

Receptionist

Muriel Phelps, we'll shampoo you now.

MURIEL EXITS TO THE SHAMPOO AREA

Cleola

What a shame. Folk don't know how to raise no 'cheerin' these days.

Sis. Patterson

Ain't that the truth. She's running around buying the child this and that and she looks a mess.

Cleola

Poor woman.

Sis. Patterson

Poor child!

DIVA DUNLAP ENTERS. SHE HAS A VERY INSECURE QUALITY ABOUT HER. SHE IS DRESSED IN SWEATS, AN OLD SWEATER AND DARK GLASSES WHICH SHE REMOVES UPON APPROACHING THE DESK.

Receptionist

Hello may I help you?

Diva

Ah, hi.

Receptionist

Hi.

Diva

Uhm, I was wondering... do you do hair weaves here?

Receptionist

Yes. We do bond weaving, braid weaving and track weaving.

Diva

How much does it cost?

Receptionist

Bond weaving involves the gluing process. It costs $175 for the hair and $190 for the process.
Braid weaving is done by actually braiding hair into your own hair. The finer the braids, the more
expensive the process. The price including the hair ranges from $375 to $800. Track weaving
involves sewing pieces of hair onto a braided section of your hair. This process ranges from
$200 to $600.

Diva

Well, what do you think?

Receptionist

I don't think you need a weave at all but if you ask me, braid weaving is best. You get more
versatility that way.

Diva

Well how much do you think it'll cost to get medium fine braids with French European way hair all over?

Receptionist

The cheapest I can tell you is $575.00 which includes perming, coloring and styling.

Diva

But I only have... I mean, I was only prepared to spend $400.

Receptionist

(aside) Well prepare yourself to keep that tired hair do then.

Diva

(to herself) Now, let's see. Maybe if I only paid half of my rent, then I could get the weave and work something out with the landlord for later in the month. Yeah, that's what I'll do.

Receptionist

Have you decided?

Diva

Yes I've decided. I'd like to go with the braid weave I asked about.

Receptionist

Very well. Name?

Diva

Diva Dunlap.

Receptionist

Ms. Dunlap, I just want to let you know that this process is not only expensive but it could take quite a bit of time. You should be prepared to spend the next eight to ten hours in the shop.

Diva

Okay. Uhm, may I use the phone?

Receptionist

Here you go.

Diva

(on the phone) Hello mama. Could you take little Jason to the doctor today for me?... I know I didn't come home last night mama. I had some things on my mind. I just had to hang out for a while... I'm at the beauty shop and I'm going to find another job soon mama... I'm gonna pay *her* too mama... I know we're behind... I know... Mama, I'm on a business phone so could you please take Jason to the doctor for me. I think I made his appointment for 3 o'clock... and could you tell him I love him... And mama, thanks for everything. I love you mama. (to receptionist) Thanks.

DIVA TURNS TO GO AND HAVE A SEAT JUST AS L.L. COOL JONES STROLLS OUT OF THE SHAMPOO AREA WEARING A PLASTIC CAP. HE SITS. THEN GRETA GUCCI COMES OUT AND GOES TO THE RECEPTIONIST TO PAY FOR HER SERVICES. AS SHE IS ABOUT TO LEAVE SHE SPOTS DIVA DUNLAP.

Greta

Denise? Denise Dunlap? Girl, is that you?

Diva

Greta? Greta Gucci? From Crenshaw High?

Greta

Yes girl, you know this is me! How have you been?

Diva

Well first of all the name is Diva now. I changed it. Y'know 'just wanted to boost up the image a little bit. Secondly, I've been.... well... I've been okay. Just okay. What about you? You look fabulous as usual.

Greta

Thanks. You know it's been the same old, same old for me.

Diva

Are you still dating that professional football player?

Greta

No honey, you know stuff gets old.

Cleola

(overhearing this, she turns to Sis. Patterson) I wonder did *his* stuff get old to her or did *her* stuff get old to him?

Sis. Patterson

(chuckles) Girl mind your business.

Greta

How about you and Roger?

Diva

Well Roger and me were fine. We had our music thing going, he cleaned up his act and then when our son was born he decided to go into a stable career so he joined the police force.

Greta

Oh, the police department has great benefits if you can just avoid the job hazard.

Diva

Well Roger didn't survive the odds one bit.... He was killed... the second day on the job.

Greta

(floored by this news and flooded with questions) Ooh no! I am so sorry to hear that.
What happened? What did you do? Are you okay? Do you need anything?

Diva

No not really. It's been a year already and I'm still trying to pull myself together. It seems like
every time I grab hold of something it just slips away. I want to have a piece of that life that
everybody talks about. I want a home for my son. I want piece in my family. I want to be a
success story but I don't know how to do it. It seems that the only thing I know how to be is
tired, broke and lonely and Lord knows I can't survive like this much longer. (She takes a beat
and collects herself.) But right now I just want to feel good about myself. I want to be *beautiful*.

Greta

But Denise, ah Diva, you are beautiful.

Diva

Yeah but I want your kind of beauty. You women seem to have it all.

GRETA THINKS ABOUT THIS BUT DOESN'T REALLY KNOW WHAT TO SAY.

Greta

...Well girl, you just hang in there okay.

Diva

Child, I'm hanging and I'm gon' keep on hanging. First I wanna start with a new look.
I want that Janet Jackson look....

Greta

Well girl you're gonna have to buy a lot of hair for that, trust me I know.

THEY LAUGH AND HUDDLE FOR MORE CHATTER WHEN WE SEE L.L. COOL JONES
CROSS TO DIVA.

L.L.

(he is showing off his cash) Excuse me Miss Lady, do you have change for a one hundred
dollar bill? I need some change for the candy machine.

Diva

Ah no, I 'm sorry I don't.

THE RECEPTIONIST SEES THAT L.L. IS HARASSING THE CUSTOMERS.

Receptionist

Oh L.L.? You can go on back. Phillip will rinse you out now. By the way would you like to buy
a candy bar from me? My nephew is trying to raise money so he can go to camp...

L.L.

Hell no. I ain't got no money for that!!

HE STRUTS OFF INTO THE SALON. MAYME ENTERS.

Receptionist

Hi maam. May I help you?

Mayme

Good afternoon, my name is Mayme Cantrell and I'd like to get my hair done.

Receptionist

(checks her book) Okay you're in luck. We just had a cancellation. What will you be having done?

Mayme

I'd like a press n'curl.

THE CHATTERING STOPS AND THERE IS UTTER SILENCE WHILE EVERYONE STARES AT HER.

Receptionist

Um, um... I'm not sure if they still do that here. I'll go check.

SHE QUICKLY EXITS. THE OTHER SALON PATRONS STOP STARING AND WHISPER AMONG THEMSELVES, "DID SHE SAY PRESS N' CURL? WHERE'S SHE BEEN? WHAT'S THE MATTER WITH HER?" OR ANY SUCH COMMENTS. THIS RING OF CHATTER IS BROKEN WHEN WE HEAR AN ARGUMENT BURSTING THROUGH THE WINGS OF THE SALON AREA. IT IS AFRIKA AND RAMON ENGAGED IN A HEATED DISCUSSION ON THE BLACK MAN. THE NEXT SERIES OF EVENTS TAKE PLACE IN RAPID SUCCESSION UP TO THE END OF ACT ONE.

Afrika

I'm telling you man, you're all wrong. As you put those chemicals of lye and dye in your hair, you not only remove the naps and kinks of your natural heritage, you are removing the rugged durability of your African American manhood!

Ramon

How are you gonna tell me about manhood when you don't even have a job *Brother!*

CLEOLA IS BREAKING HER NECK TRYING TO HEAR THIS WHEN SIS. PATTERSON WHISPERS TO HER.

Sis Patterson

Come on now sister. Let them work it out. Don't be so nosy.

Cleola

(loud and defensive, this is the one bit of truth that she can't take) Who are you calling nosy? 'Much money as you spend on clothes, you don't need to be telling nobody nothing!!

Mrs. Phelps

(to Cleola) Calm down honey. I don't think she meant any harm by it.

Cleola

Now I know you're not trying to tell me nothing with your wig wearing, outta shape, can't raise no cheerin' self!

Mrs. Phelps

(upset at first, then decides to refrain) You know something, I feel sorry for people like you. The slightest little thing just brings out the nigger in you.

JUST AS WE SEE THE RECEPTIONIST USHER IN A TEARFUL MURIEL PHELPS WHOSE HAIR APPEARS TO HAVE BEEN CUT DRASTICALLY.

Muriel.

Mama, she cut my hair.

MRS. PHELPS RISES IN A FURY.

Mrs. Phelps

(she's about to 'go there') I know y'all didn't cut my baby's hair after all I went through to grow it. It's gon' be some sh*t up in here if y'all cut my baby's hair! We asked for a trim! Don't y'all know the difference between a cut and a trim?

Greta

(to Diva) Girl I got to go it's getting hot up in here and I gotta go generate some heat of my own. (her cell phone rings as she crosses towards the reception desk.) Hello, oh Hi baby.

THE RECEPTIONIST RETURNS TO HER DESK.

Receptionist

(to Mayme) 'Sorry it took so long. There is someone here that can give you a press n' curl but you're going to have to wait a while....

GRETA IS STILL ON THE PHONE BUT APPROACHES THE RECEPTIONIST TO BOOK ANOTHER APPOINTMENT. THE RECEPTIONIST GETS A CALL ON HER PHONE AS WELL. THEY ARE BOTH TALKING ON THE PHONE AND TO EACH OTHER AS WELL.

Greta

(on the phone) Oh really? (to the receptionist) I needs to make an appointment for two weeks from now. (on the phone) Ah, huh I know. (to the receptionist) Do you have anything?

THEN WE SEE HEAR A PAGER GO OFF. AT THE SOUND OF THIS WE SEE THAT L.L. HAS READ THE NUMBER ON THE PAGER AND IS HURRIEDLY ATTEMPTING TO RETURN THE CALL ON HIS CELL PHONE.

L.L.

(regarding his phone) It's dead! The battery is dead. I knew I should have charged it! I gotta find a phone. This is urgent, money is on the line, I Got To Find A Phone!

HE SCOPES THE PLACE AND SEES GRETA AT THE FRONT DESK ON HER PHONE.

L.L.

Excuse me Miss but yo, can I use your phone?

GRETA GIVES HIM A SERIOUS LOOK AND KEEPS TALKING.

L.L.

Yo B*tch, I told you I need that phone now!

DIVA RISES AND SLOWLY CROSSES TO THE RECEPTION DESK.

Greta

Listen here you little sub-human, ghettofied orphaned, welfare reject you better watch who you're talking to cause I just might carry more than make up in my purse!

DIVA

(to receptionist) Look I just came here to get my hair weaved...

AT THE HEIGHT OF THIS COMMOTION MAYME SPEAKS.

MAYME

Stop!!!!

THEY ALL STARE IN AMAZEMENT AND FREEZE IN PLACE. LIGHTS OUT.

END OF ACT ONE.

Act Two:

THE ACTORS RESET IN THE SAME FROZEN POSITIONS. LIGHTS UP THEN THE
COMMOTION RESUMES. THE SHOP IS IN UTTER CHAOS. MAYME SPEAKS AGAIN
THIS TIME LIKE THE CRACK OF THUNDER.

Mayme

Stop!!! All of you stop it! I can't believe the things I hear coming from my so called people.

Greta

Uhmp, and who are you?

Mayme

I'm Mayme Cantrell and I have worked as an undercover security agent in this mall for fifteen years
and believe it or not, I know all of you.

THEY REACT.

Mayme

(continues) Oh maybe not my name... (to L.L.) or booking number in some cases but I know you.
I've walked right beside you, peeped your conversations and observed you when you didn't even
know you were being watched. Oh I'm proud that I didn't find any thieves...

SHE WALKS AROUND THE ROOM WITH AUTHORITY.

Mayme

Instead I found the opposite. I found a people that were so quietly being robbed of their
pride, spirit and culture that they didn't even know it. (to L.L.) What's your name son?

L.L.

My name is L.L. Cool Jones.

Mayme

What's your NAME boy?

L.L.

(sheepishly) Ah Gabriel Sims.

Mayme

Gabriel. Your mama named you after an angel to be an example, a leader... instead you're around
here bobbing and swaying drenched in gold chains wearing symbols of ignorance and consumption!

L.L.

Hey why you frontin' on me? What's your trip old lady?

Mayme

I'm frontin' on you because I care about you and I ain't scared of you! If you shot me
dead right now, then I died a worthwhile death cause I *died* trying to give a young brother
a shot of wisdom. Now are your boys gon' do that for you?

L.L.

Look I'm just trying to get paid that's all, I gots to get PAID!

Mayme

And where does your money go... back into the fast suicidal life that produced it in the first place?
And how long do you think you're gonna gamble before either a prison cell or a bullet come up with
your name on it? Say no to that lifestyle young man, say no...

L.L.

Well how am I supposed to say no when to this very day my mama, my sisters and my brothers is still
on welfare. How I'm gon' say no when my daddy left long before I even learned how to pronounce the
word 'daddy.' How am I gon' say no when it's either this or minimum wage or seeing my mama
work herself to death and still never get ahead? 'And you want me to just say NO!

Mayme

Damn straight! I want you to just say no! Have you forgotten or did you even know that our
ancestors faced more obstacles than we could ever imagine and still they helped build this and many
nations. They didn't sell out and neither can we. If you're dead or in jail your seed will not grow.
You will not be there to procreate and raise up the next generation! Now I know you love your mama
but she won't be the first mama to work hard to provide for her children and the *longest* day at work is
better than the shortest day at the funeral home! If you want to meet a real challenge then rise to the
occasion of carving out a decent and honorable life. As for your father, I know that black men have
been down trodden through the years and I don't excuse any man for turning his back on his family but
you have it within you to be the kind of father that you always wanted to have.

L.L. LOOKS AS THOUGH HE'D LIKE TO RESPOND BUT HE DOESN'T KNOW HOW. HE STARES FOR A MOMENT AND THEN EXITS.

                              Mrs. Phelps

That's right. Tell that boy right!

                              Mayme

Mrs. Phelps, right?

MRS. PHELPS IS SURPRISED THAT MAYME KNOWS HER.

                              Mayme

A few years ago your daughter got lost in the mall and you had her paged. I'll never forget that worried look on your face and the relief when we located Muriel. I sort of kept track of you over the years. You really are a caring mother.

                              Mrs. Phelps

Why thanks, I try. Y' know it's not easy working and raising a child.

                              Mayme

I know and I've seen you do some of everything for this child except *listen* to her.

                              Mrs. Phelps

Now excuse me but....

                              Mayme

No, excuse me. I'm a mother too and I know that pretty clothes and music lessons are fine but when the child needs to know the truth about sex and drugs Beethoven and Tommy Wear can't help her. 'Seems like you're so busy making her into the dream you never lived that you don't even know who she is or who you are. When was the last time you did something to make you happy? (regarding her wig) I'm sure your scalp would like to breathe once in a while. God knows you deserve it.

Muriel

(lovingly) Yes mama.

Mayme

You focus on the beauty and promise of Muriel as if your life is completely over. You're a beautiful lady and it's time to let your hair down again.

Mrs. Phelps

(after a long stare) Miss, I think it is a bit forward of you to take such liberties and voice your opinions about me, my child and my life... but I'm glad you did.

Ramon

(stands in defiance) I've got to go. I feel like I just stepped into the studio audience of a TV talk show!

HE CROSSES TO THE DESK. MRS. PHELPS AND MURIEL PAY THE RECEPTIONIST AND LEAVE.

Mayme

Ramon! Ramon Reeves!

Ramon

(defensively) How do you know who.....

Mayme

The man all the ladies just can't seem to resist.

Ramon

(flattered) It's not my fault if they can't control their hormones. And what business is it of yours?

Mayme

In my years of patrolling these stores, I've heard your name a time or two. I've also seen you sporting some of L.A.'s finest You got class you got style and you love to show off your lovely ladies day after day, week after week right here in the neon corridors of this mall.

Ramon

Yeah, and....

Mayme

I've seen you with so many different women I had to ask myself is this one man keeping all of these women happy and do they know about each other? No, it's none of my business but you might be wise to stop using your body like a toy and women as your playthings. You take it for granted that God has blessed youth with good looks, a good job and a good education but you've got to remember that black men and black women have suffered through the ages so that you can march your suave behind around here like you're doing the rest of us a favor..

Ramon

Look! You don't understand! Women just....

Mayme

As long as you're alive you have a choice! Aids is killing us in record numbers. The family structure is under attack! And just because you have the potential to be a good catch doesn't make it right for you to be a career Casanova. If you keep it up then one day you're gonna wake up old and lonely in a big house with a BMW in the garage... and *if* there's a woman beside you you're gonna wonder if she really loves you or your car. Pretty faces and hot bodies are a dime a dozen. Love is what's real. You'll find that out some day if you happen to loose your good looks and money. You might not think you need anybody now but one day you will.

RAMON STARES AT HER FOR A MOMENT

Ramon

I gotta go!

HE CHARGES OFF THROWING HIS MONEY AT THE COUNTER.

Afrika

(jumps up) Right on sister! Right on! I am so glad that somebody has got some sense around here. I was trying to tell that brother that his head is all screwed up. He got them chemicals in his hair... getting them sissy manicures. He's gone off the deep end ain't he?

AT THIS POINT HE NOTICES THAT HE'S BEEN CARRYING ON ALL BY HIMSELF AND THAT MAYME HAS JUST BEEN STARING AT HIM.

Afrika

(continuing) As-Salaam-Alaikum.

Mayme

(warmly amused) Wa-Likum-Salaam. Now, I hate to be the one to break it to you but just cause you're walking around here funky under the arms wearing a dashiki and an afro doesn't mean you're any blacker than the rest of us it does mean that you could use a little right guard.

Afrika

Hey, wait a minute sister, the white man's got your brain messed up to.

Mayme

You tell me what in the world has the white man have to do with the fact that you don't work?

Afrika

How you know what I do?

Mayme

I see you here three or four times a week hanging 'round smoking cigarettes, wearing out the concrete.

BEAT.

Mayme

(continuing) I think you've even held a few jobs here.

Afrika

These redneck people her are all the same...

Mayme

Now wait a minute we also have several black owned businesses right here in this mall and if you can't work for them then who can you work for, huh?

Afrika

(weakening) It's not just them... it's the system... it's the economy... it's the women... it's....

Mayme

What's your name honey?

Afrika

Afrika.

Mayme

(aside) If you say so. (to Afrika) Afrika, it may be all those things but you may be better off here than in the mother land. Stand up for your fights, fight for the cause but remember this is America and this is where you live and breath, so until you find another home, this is your home.

Afrika

(confused) I just don't know sometimes. I'm a good person but I'm confused. I want to make things work but they always seem to explode!

Mayme

That's because you're looking to the future but you're living in the past. Look at you baby, it's not 1973 anymore.

AFRIKA LOOKS DOWN AT HIMSELF.

                              Afrika

It's not?

                              Mayme

Nooo. Listen, I believe that you can make a difference but sometimes you just come off so strong that you scare people away. You try to teach but you failed to learn. You want to lead but you've never followed.

AFRIKA'S HEAD IS HANGING LOW AND HE SLOWLY PACES OUT.

                              Afrika

(to receptionist) Here's my money for my hair cut.

                              Mayme

(reaching after him) Afrika you can have that woman you desire too.

                              Afrika

(with pleasant disbelief) A woman?

                              Mayme

But you can't rule her. A woman that has anything to offer you will be a woman of substance but remember she came from your rib not your feet.

AFRIKA EXITS. EVERYONE ELSE HAS BEEN WATCHING AND LISTENING.
AS AFRIKA EXITS LIGHT CHATTER BEGINS AGAIN.

                              Mayme

(to receptionist) I didn't come here to say all of this. I just came to get my hair done.
How long do you think it'll take...

CLEOLA JUMPS UP AND MARCHES TO THE RECEPTION DESK.

Cleola

(to receptionist) Excuse me but honey I got to go. I've been sitting here all day. I can't go outta here looking like don King. These hair dressers charge all that money and all they do is stand around talking about *everybody's* business.

THERE IS SILENCE WHILE EVERYONE STARES AT CLEOLA.

Cleola

Why are y'all looking at me like that?

THE STARES GROW EVEN BIGGER.

Cleola

Are y'all trying to say I *talk too much?*

All

TOO MUCH!

Cleola

(Appalled) So now I know who my real friends are. Petunia you too?

Sis. Patterson

Cleola, you seem like a nice lady but when we met you already knew everything about me.

Greta

Me too.

Cleola

(to Mayme) Now I just know you've got a handle on this one too.
What does all of this mean?

Mayme

It means that if you spent as much time managing your own affairs as you do keeping up with everybody else's then you'd be much better off.

CLEOLA BEGINS TO TAKE OFFENSE.

Mayme

Before you get all bent out of shape, remember you just asked for my opinion. Now please understand that a person like you is probably very observant and able to get people to confide in you. Don't throw those qualities away on hot tips and juicy gossip. Our people young and old need guidance and inspiration. Let someone else back stab and cut us down, we don't need to do that to ourselves.

CLEOLA CONTEMPLATES AND THEN RESPONDS AMICABLY.

Cleola

How the hell did you get to be so damn smart? (beat) Honey thank you very much! I got a new idea. Maybe I'll write a book or better yet... an advice column "Ask Cleola." Wait a minute, do you think I could be the new talk show queen? Shoot! (to receptionist) Here honey, here's my check. I'll wear it straight today. I gotta go find an agent!

CLEOLA AND MAYME EXCHANGE A FEW CHUCKLES AND THEN CLEOLA EXITS.

Receptionist

Mrs. Patterson, please report to your operator for comb out.

SIS PATTERSON RISES BUT FIRST SHE SPEAKS TO MAYME.

Sis. Patterson

(to Mayme) How are you doing ma'am. I'm Sis. Petunia Patterson and I gotta tell ya, you really have some good words to say. Here's my card. If you're ever in the neighborhood, stop by my church sometimes.

Mayme

(kindly accepts) Thank you. (She rises while searching for her card.) Y'know I'm really excited about some of the things I've been learning lately. All these years I hadn't given a second thought as to where my money was going so I started doing some financial consulting part time...

Sis. Patterson

(sweetly declines) Oh noooo thank you. I'm doing fine in that area. I've got every credit card in the book, a closet full of new clothes, a brand new Cadillac and the rent on our two bedroom apartment is paid three whole months in advance.

MAYME HOLDS ON TO HER CARD AND CONTINUES TO TALK WITH SIS. PATTERSON.

Mayme

That's great but Sis. Patterson how would you like to have all that and some property to go with it. How about a beautiful yard with rows of petunias lining the walk way of your new home? I'm sure you've got an impressive closet Ms. Patterson but is it really earning you anything but compliments? Now for your luxurious home, you can be earning equity while you sleep.

Sis. Patterson

But how am I gonna afford a house? A house isn't everybody's ultimate dream.

Mayme

That's true but you're already making somebody else a profit every time you pay the high interest rates on those credit cards. When you have five hundred dollars saved in the bank you only earn about five percent interest but when you owe five hundred dollars to the same bank you could pay anywhere from eleven to twenty percent interest on the same five hundred dollars!

Sis. Patterson

I never thought about it like that.

Mayme

Shoot, you could put a down payment on a house and a new hat collection.

Sis. Patterson

Did you say new hat collection?   Give me that card.   I'm on my way to the homeowners association dressed in style!

SIS. PATTERSON EXITS. MAYME RETURNS TO HER SEAT. DIVA AND GRETA ARE LEFT IN THE WAITING AREA. DIVA LOOKS STRESSED. GRETA'S LOOKS DEFINITELY SUGGEST THAT SHE IS NOT TO BE BOTHERED.

Greta

(blurting out to Mayme) You really gonna get a press n'curl?

Mayme

(taken aback) Yes.

Greta

But all that talk about living in the past and look at you.   You're living in the past.

Mayme

Because I want a press n' curl, I'm living in the past?

Greta

Well... yes... in a way!

Mayme

What difference does it make?

Greta

Look I don't mean to come off wrong but there's just so much more that we can make of ourselves than just a press n' curl. (to herself) Slinging all that grease and burning up your neck and ears with a straightening comb.

Mayme

You're right. There is a lot we can make of ourselves but it doesn't begin and end with our choice of hairstyle. I have fine hair that doesn't take too kindly to chemicals but that's beside the point. My press n' curl makes me feel just as good as your greased, fried and laid to the side. It's on the inside that I feel good. I don't have to go in debt or sit for nine to ten hours to have someone else's hair sewn or glued into mine to make me feel beautiful, nor do I have to wear designer cuts and chemicals to fit in with what's expected of me. Half the products we use in the name of blackness are made by somebody else anyway. It's another case of *them* telling *us* how to be *us.*

Greta

Well with that attitude, we may as well walk around bare footed with nappy hair singing Go Down Moses.

Mayme

I'm not knocking hair dye, chemicals, cuts, curls or weaves for that matter but if you missed the point on everything else, understand this: whatever you put on the outside should only compliment, not supplement, the already together and beautiful person that you are. We've got babies walking around in high priced designer shoes who don't even have a college fund or trust fund. I know people who would beg, borrow or steal to have the latest fashion.

Greta

I know someone like that.

Mayme

I know some women who would share their bodies with any man if he makes enough money to support their lifestyle.

Greta

I know someone like that too.

Mayme

And if you stripped their facade, you'd find a person who was just as empty and insecure as they are glamorous...

Greta

I really know someone like that.

Mayme

Decked out on the outside, tripped out on the inside.

Greta

But life doesn't treat everybody the same. I wish I could be more educated but some people have more advantages from the start.

Mayme

You're right again but I'll bet that for the price of half the clothes in your closet you could've paid for a semester at a community college... and for the price of those beautiful shoes you could buy a self help book and for free you can study in the public library and learn about your rich cultural past. And if it's spiritual guidance that you're needing, I don't know a church, mosque or temple in this city that charges admission. So what are you waiting for?

THE RECEPTION DESK PHONE RINGS. THE RECEPTIONIST ANSWERS. GRETA SITS AND THINKS FOR A MOMENT.

Greta

I... I um... I'd better go. I got a date, um, I've got an appointment to get to. (she hugs Diva) Take care of yourself girl. Call me. (She scribbles her number and crosses to the front desk.) I'll see you next week.

GRETA EXITS. RECEPTIONIST HANGS UP THE PHONE.

Receptionist

Mrs. Cantrell you may go back now.

MAYME EXITS. DIVA SITS AND PONDERS ALL THAT SHE HAS HEARD. THE FRONT DESK PHONE RINGS AGAIN. RECEPTIONIST ANSWERS. SHE TALKS BRIEFLY AND THEN HOLDS THE PHONE IN HER HAND.

Receptionist

(into the telephone) Just a minute. (to Diva) Ms. Dunlap, could you step up to the desk please.

DIVA CROSSES TO THE DESK

Receptionist

Your hair operator has just informed me that she's out of the kind of hair that you requested but she does have Brazilian Wavy. It looks almost the same but costs a little less. So the cost would only be $525.00. Of course we'd have to put an extra strong perm on your hair so that the two textures will match but trust me you will look beautiful. Will that be okay?

DIVA STANDS THERE WITH NO RESPONSE.

Receptionist

(into the telephone) Okay. (to Diva) She said she'll knock twenty five dollars off the price... (listens to the phone) uh, uhm, okay. (to Diva) She said that she'll even come out here and show you her weave so you'll know that it looks natural. (to the phone) Okay. (to Diva) She said you'll look just like Janet Jackson.

DIVA STILL STANDS WITH NO RESPONSE.

Receptionist

(very annoyed at this point) Miss Dunlap, do you want this here hair weave or WHAT?!

LIGHTS OUT.

END OF ACT TWO.

The End

ORDER FORM

Fax Orders (818) 942-2205 ext. 0016   **On Line Orders www.sea2sun.com**

                              Postal Orders: Sea To Sun Books
                                           13547 Ventura Blvd. #678
SAN: 2 5 3 - 9 5 5 1   **Sherman Oaks, Ca. 91423**
                                           (818) 942-2205 ext. 0016

Name: _____

_____
(Please list if you are a Performer, Professor, Book Store or Professional coach.)

Address: _____

City: _____   State: _____   Zip: _____

Telephone: _____   E-mail: _____

Please send _____ copies of Dictation at $ 24.95 each.   Book(s) $ _____

Shipping and Handling: $3.00 for first book
and $1.00 for each additional book.   Shipping $ _____

Sales Tax: 8 %   Sales Tax $ _____

                                                            Grand Total: $ _____

Payment: Make checks or money orders payable to: Sea To Sun Books

_____ Visa   _____ Mastercard   Card # _____

         Expiration Date: _____

Please allow four to six weeks for delivery. Thank you for our order.

Good luck with your career!